Connect Money and Soul

Create the Life You Want

Sarah Swales

Connect Money and Soul

Create the Life you Want

Copyright: © 2022 by Sarah J. Swales.

TXu 2-266-036

Effective date of Registration: June 22, 2021

All rights reserved.

v.1.3

No part of this book may be reproduced in any way or form or by any mechanical means including information storage and retrieval systems without permission in writing from the publisher/author, except by a reviewer who may quote passages in a review.

Front cover: photo by SretaZi

Category: Self-help/Decision-making, self-knowledge, personal finance.

Quantity Purchases: Schools, companies, professional groups, clubs, and other organizations may qualify for special terms when ordering quantities of the title. For information, email; sarahjaneswales@gmail.com or visit my website at sarahswales.wordpress.com

All rights reserved by Sarah J. Swales and Bamboo Press.

This book is printed in the United States of America.

BAMBOO PRESS

Dedication

For
Colin, William, and Henry

Contents

		Page
Introduction		1
Chapter 1	The Groundwork	5
Chapter 2	The Big Picture	23
Chapter 3	Rekindle Life-Force	57
Chapter 4	Your Money Psychology	105
Chapter 5	Your Financial Picture	145
Chapter 6	Financial Strategies	159
Chapter 7	Investing	185
Chapter 8	Important Questions	207
Chapter 9	Making It Happen	219
Chapter 10	Case Studies	231

Introduction

Are you winning the life-long "tug of war" between money and your soul?

This book will guide you towards the life you yearn for, with your soul and your money in sync.

It may seem odd to group ideas of self-actualization and financial security together. But it turns out you can't have one without the other. They are interdependent no matter where you are on the financial spectrum and no matter how clearly you are able (or not) to see your way ahead.

The choices we make, (or don't make) and the reality we create, matter exponentially as they either reinforce or contradict the very essence of who we are.

The choices we make matter!

One unconsidered choice can lead to another and another until we wake up one day wondering who we are, and how we have arrived in the wrong place, living the wrong life!

A glimpse at my background may explain how I became so fascinated by the money/soul relationship. My two primary careers have been: Financial Planner and Yoga Instructor!

Over years as a Financial Planner, I listened to my clients' stories, and this is what I frequently heard:

"The persistent financial demands of daily life gradually chipped away at who I once was, and the life I had dreamed of - until I lost sight of the dream".

As we juggle money and authenticity a sense of alienation can arise. Staying true to who we are, to what we value, *and* finding our financial comfort zone can seem impossible. It is all too easy to compromise either our dreams or our financial security. If we take care of *either* our money *or* our soul, over time a gaping hole will appear between them. The tug of war arises and eventually, either one or the other loses the war and withers.

My purpose is to reunite money and your soul. To reawaken your connection to self, and to your desire, *and* adjust your relationship with money so that each of life's transitions is greeted with integrity, delight, and no stress.

The purpose of this book is to unpeel the grip of money from around your soul and set your money and your soul free.

Making peace between your soul and money is no mean feat. It requires introspection, honesty, and courage. Above all, it requires the ability to meet the not inconsiderable challenge of change, when change is necessary.

There are three essential components to creating the life you want with the money you have:

Discovering your Self.

Rekindling your desires and values.

Reconciling the sometimes-opposing pulls of financial security, and desire.

There are 4 parts to this book:

First, we consider practices that are essential for understanding yourself and your relationship with money.

Second, we look at where you are now, the details of your life, and the importance of reawakening what *you want* and acknowledging what is waiting to happen.

Third, we focus on all aspects of money: How you feel about it, how you organize it, and what you do with it! We delve into the workings of money alone. We weave in the interplay of the Self as it dances with both money and desire.

Finally, we see how others have managed to connect money and their soul to create the life they love. The case studies in Chapter 10 may be read independently from the rest of the book at any time.

I use both ideas and exercises throughout the process. It is best to read the chapters in the order they are presented but the exercises may take days or weeks to complete so there are a couple of ways to proceed:

- Read the book straight through. Then re-read each chapter and work on the exercises as you read for the second time.
- Or do the exercises as they occur and review the previous chapters as you do them.

The financial sections are not necessarily intended for sophisticated investors but hopefully, there will be information that helps everyone when moving toward a life change.

I am fully aware that change is a luxury that is very scarce for millions of people. For those born into abject poverty, or those suffering from ill health, there may be little, or no possibility of change and our hearts go out to them. However, I would argue that for those of us who do have the opportunity to make change for the betterment of ourselves *and* others, then this opportunity should not be wasted. And if we use that luxury as best we can, maybe some of us will feel drawn to help those less fortunate than ourselves.

Are you ready for a profound change to your life? Well then, let's get to it!

Chapter 1 - *The Groundwork*

Let's start by considering practices that help you look afresh at yourself, your life, and your relationship with money. These practices reveal if the path you currently tread is truly *your* path—to see if it aligns with your heart's desire *and* your need for financial security.

These practices will help you recognize what brings you alive and inspires you, and what stifles and perhaps scares you. They will keep you alert to each emotional shift, as you move through your days. They will keep you from becoming distracted and lead you toward a deeper awareness of life as it unfolds and change if it calls.

Most of the practices I'm referring to derive in some way from ancient philosophies that were brought into the mainstream in 1979 by Jon Kabat-Zinn when he developed the concept of Mindfulness. I want to show you how to use them specifically to examine how money and your soul interact. Part of this process is to reach acceptance of where you are now and then move gracefully into what is coming next.

The techniques include:

- Learning to Witness
- Learning to be present
- Learning from your physical being

1. The Witness

We, as humans, tend to experience life as meaningful when we know and express what we love about ourselves- our unique individuality. As we start to question how we want our life to be, we must first come to understand that uniqueness and develop a sweet intimacy with it.

A fundamental tool to help you do this is often referred to as the Witness. The Witness is the part of you that watches yourself in a neutral, dispassionate, and non-judgmental way as you move through your days.

When your Witness is alive, you observe the internal workings of your mind, notice everything you think, feel, and do, from a slight remove- as if you were sitting on your own shoulder!

It is as if you were a character in a movie, but you are also *watching* the movie, detached from it. The Witness notices each action, shift in energy, each mood, and emotion, and the endless flow of thoughts. Being the audience as well as the actor in the movie prevents you from becoming "lost" in it. You are simply fully aware of it. Free to enjoy it, the fun bits *and* the hard bits!

"Thought is like a little loom shuttle which is always going to and fro, and to be freed from its tyrannical motion is to step out of a prison into the open air."

A Search in Secret India. Paul Brunton

The Witness teaches us that everything we experience will eventually soften, move through, and dissipate.

Dwelling in Witness allows us to take a breath before responding to any given situation. And as we breathe, we can learn to "name and tame" difficult thoughts or feelings. We learn to accept them and wait for them to pass. When they pass, we may learn to calmly trace the emotion to its source- and understand how it has contributed to who we have become.

I'll share a personal example. As an only child, my greatest fear was to be left out. When I felt left out, I would react to the pain in one of two ways. Either I would feel sorry for myself, or I would act out, show off, boast—anything to get attention and seem special enough to be included!

Eventually, I was able to step back from the pain of those moments to see how it was affecting my behavior and trace the pain back to its source. As I named the pain, it began to lose its sting. I was able to see that my reactive behavior was my defense, that I was compensating for what I felt I lacked. Gradually, I was able to accept my vulnerability and stop hiding behind a mask of bravado or self-pity. I was able to move closer to the people whose company I desired.

As you start to use your Witness, you too will start to recognize repeated patterns of behavior and emotion and understand them. You will start to understand their genesis. Gradually you will realize that how you react is a choice. You will move towards greater authenticity.

Each step on the path of self-knowledge will help you with each decision you make. It will become easier to align your decisions with what you know to be true about yourself. You will become the author of your own story.

You may feel that all this "inner reflection" is akin to "navel-gazing" and self-obsession, but in fact, the reverse is true. When we are not consumed by, and fused with our own thoughts and feelings, but merely watching them, our minds become clearer. We become more receptive and open to ourselves and to others.

Here are some practices to help you integrate the Witness into your everyday life.

Awaken the Witness

a. Cultivate the habit of simply **stopping** for just a few minutes, several times a day. Stop whatever you're doing and relax. Then spend the next moment noticing, taking stock. Watch your breath gently move in and out, and notice your thoughts, feelings, your mood, and your energy level. See if you can observe without the need to fix or change anything. The mind may start having opinions and that's OK, but during these few moments of stillness, try to stay with your experience as it is. Notice yourself truly *being* without doing, and feel the joy of being.

b. Sit comfortably and bring your attention to your breath. You may notice how your mind is thinking, judging, and wandering. That's what the mind does! Then begin to moderate your breath by silently counting to 3 on the inhalation, and to 4 on the exhalation. The silent counting will help your mind become more focused and calm. Keep counting until you notice that your mind has wandered and, that you are following your thoughts rather than observing them. Name what you are thinking, be it work, dinner, a movie, the kids, etc. Just name and accept it. Each time you do this, be curious about where your mind wanders. Notice the intensity and quality of your thoughts and if they create a reaction, either physical or emotional. Then return to the breath and start counting again. Begin this practice for just 5 minutes at a time.

c. Eventually practice this awareness of your thoughts as you move through the day. At first, you may set an intention to watch your thoughts for half an hour, then an hour, and so on. Keep doing what you do in your daily life. Keep having conversations, eating meals, doing your work, meeting friends, and exercising. See if you can keep a little part of yourself at a distance by watching your thoughts, and your emotions, watching your reactions as the "movie" runs and runs. Before you go to bed, you might ask yourself, "What did I learn from my movie today?" The more that you can observe the workings of the mind, the more you become intimate with what moves and enthralls you. And the more you will become aware of the role money plays in your life.

2. Presence

Moments of Presence arise when the mind is sufficiently quiet. Awareness of everything and everyone around you becomes heightened. All five senses are alive. You are fully experiencing life, not dulling it behind the crescendo of the mind. Whatever the nature of the events that are happening, their depth and richness expand.

"Presence is the greatest gift we can give ourselves and others. Presence means that our awareness is focused on the current moment, with no concern for the future or the past. Mind chatter is at a minimum, leaving us alert, sensitive, and responsive".

Your Presence is Enough. Julia Tindall

This means that as you sip your tea you not only enjoy the warmth and taste of the tea but the cool smoothness of the cup against your lip! It means that as you stand under the shower you feel individual drops of hot water as they slide down your back. It means that as you listen to your friend speak, your attention is on the meaning behind each of his words, not your own ideas on the topic. As Ellen Langer so aptly puts it:

"Whatever you're doing, do it."

Mindfulness. Ellen Langer

As obvious as this may seem, I have found myself, over the years, in many quite heated discussions on the feasibility and even the advisability of Presence. People will ask: "How can I be in the present moment and simultaneously contemplate my future as you are suggesting we do in this book? That's a contradiction! The very idea of the future is contrary to what's happening right now!"

There is no contradiction. The seed of the next action resides in the present action. Or, as Eckhart Tolle puts it:

"The quality of your consciousness at this moment is what shapes your future".

A New Earth: Awakening to Your Life's Purpose. Eckhart Tolle

Without Presence, we can only stumble blindly into the future. How can we possibly see our way forward, or what we really want unless we experience life as it happens? If we show up now, if we feel what we feel as it unfolds, then we can know what parts of that we want to carry forward. And what parts we no longer need. As we experience joy in the present, we know that we can carry the source of that joy into the future. What is happening now is the only thing we can know. It is the source of inspiration that will define the next moments.

A second question that arises is this: "My mind is my most valuable asset. How can you suggest that I ignore the amazing workings of my brain and strive for a quiet mind'?"

Again, there is no contradiction. There is, however, a difference between conscious thought and unconscious mind "babble". Our minds are indeed amazing instruments and when used consciously to pay attention, to solve problems, to create, to bask in the delight of another person, they are at their best. But when left to their own devices, unconsciously, the mind leaps randomly from thought to thought, each thought lost in the next! Try to become aware of the difference.

And finally, this question:

"Sometimes I drop so deeply into an activity that I literally *become* the activity I am engaged in. My attention is completely absorbed. I am no longer painting, I *become* painting. There seems to be no distinction between me and the activity, I am simply lost in it. I feel in these moments that I am totally present, but how can this be, if I am lost, unaware of anything else?"

Again, I suggest that there is no contradiction. You are indeed present when totally absorbed in that way. There is no distraction, there is no mind babble. The difference is that during those times, your Witness is mostly quiet. The Witness may only awaken periodically, to notice that **you** are totally focused and present. There is a subtle difference between being present and becoming conscious of your presence simultaneously when the Witness is more active.

Our Witness and our ability to drop into Presence are essential tools to fully participate in the precious years we have been given. They are essential tools if we are to truly know ourselves and move through a life that is the highest expression and enjoyment of that self.

This is because nestled at the center of each moment of Presence *is* our Unique Self. It is in moments of Presence that we can touch our essence.

Then, as we meet each decision and choice in life, this sense of self guides us toward our most fulfilling path.

Ellen Langer describes those who lack these tools like this:

"They're not there and they're not there to know they're not there!"

Counterclockwise. Ellen Langer

One such moment of self-awareness has always stayed with me. I was walking down a road, returning from an errand. Suddenly I emerged from the endless chitter chatter of my brain into my surroundings and stepped into Presence. I felt the sidewalk beneath my feet, I saw each link of the fence to my left, I felt the sun on my skin, the hum of the cars passing. My walk to the store had become a rich sensual feast.

And in that moment of Presence, I experienced a deep sense of Self. There were no words to describe "who I am", just a fundamental sense of Me!

No words are needed to feel who you are!

Think back to times when you have had such an experience.

The Practice of Presence is fundamental to our quest of navigating life with authenticity, joy, and passion.

Here are ways to practice:

Practice Presence:

a. Practice Presence through your senses.

Our senses are a delightful gateway to Presence. Pick a time when you can be alone and pick a place that is powerfully sensual for you. This could be in a hot candlelit bath, it could be on a secret park bench, on a forest trail, by (or in) the ocean, lake, or river even on a busy subway train in the city. It could be curled up in bed, or running through wet grass barefoot, skiing on pristine snow while it is snowing. In fact, any moment, anywhere, anytime, is perfect. Hold the intention of presence and awaken each of your senses. Smell the air, feel it on your skin, feel, even taste the rain, the snow, the sun, the air. See the intensity of each flower, each tree trunk, and delight in all the sounds that surround you: birds, traffic, voices, whatever bombards each sense. Feel it, hear it, taste it, see it, smell it. Sometimes all this is enough to quell the voice in the head and free you to be available to life, as it is happening.

When you return, write down everything you remember from your experience and what stands out most powerfully in your memory. I tried this recently on a run. There were long blank periods where I had slipped from presence and drifted off into unconscious thought (which I could not remember). I couldn't even remember the route I had taken during the blank times!

Here is part of what I wrote:

Powerful smell of acrid tar destined for road surface,

Piercing caw of greedy crow demanding his share,

Eyes drawn to Hi-Viz orange vest of workman

Topped by a beaming, quite round, black face.

"Wonderful weather" he grins as I jog past.

Now there's a point of view.

Blank.

Unknown numbers of moments

Lost in unheard babble of the mind...etc.

And so it goes. Watch out! Life is easy to miss.

b. Being Present with others:

"Let others see their own greatness when looking into your eyes"

Walking with Justice. Mollie Marti J.D. Ph.D.

Being present with others is one of the greatest gifts you can give...to them and to yourself. When interacting with others, set the intention of Presence. Ask questions and listen closely to what they say. Give them the gift of attention. Ask for more detail, clarification, and explanation. Often when we "listen" we are flipping through the files in our own head for some of our own stories to share. Resist that temptation. Stay with *their* topic, explore how they feel, go deeper. This is not easy and requires a great deal of presence to not interject your own opinions, information and stories. In other words, to direct the conversation back to yourself. If you can soften the need to be heard there is the possibility of finding not only a deeper sense of connection with the other... but also, with yourself. Offer the gift of allowing someone to feel truly seen and heard.

Can you tell, as you move through your days, which of the people you meet are present and which are not? How would you describe the difference?

3. Listen to your Body

The union of mind and body is now indisputable and any serious self-inquiry should honor that fact. Often the body delivers your truth more directly than the convoluted messages from the mind. You must pay close attention to the body as you explore your emotional self and endeavor to know yourself better.

Dr Candace Pert, a neuropharmacologist who worked at the NIH and Georgetown University Medical Center, is renowned for her work in this field. In "The Molecules of Emotion, The Science behind Mind-Body Medicine" she states:

"Your body is your subconscious mind".

Emotions trigger the release of special compounds known as peptides that are stored in the body, whether in tissue, organ, or muscle. It is Dr. Pert's (and many others') contention that every part of your body is therefore potentially a storage place for your emotional reaction. Pert continues:

"A feeling sparked in our mind or body will translate as a peptide being released somewhere. Organ, tissues, skin, muscle, and endocrine glands all have peptide receptors on them and can access and store emotional information. This means the emotional *memory is stored in many places in the body, not just or even primarily, in the brain. You can access emotional memory anywhere in the peptide/receptor network, in any number of ways. I think unexpressed emotions are literally lodged in the body. The real true emotions that need to be expressed are in the body, trying to move up and be expressed and thereby integrated, made whole, and healed."*

Information revealed by your physical being is invaluable when getting to know yourself, your life, and your relationship to money.

And as your truth begins to surface, your first reaction may be to deny it. You may fear that the truth will cause upheaval, disarray, even possible conflict. But unfortunately, it seems that if you don't pay attention to emotions, if you do just bury them, eventually they make themselves heard with aches and pains, rashes, inflammations, and conflict with loved ones. If something is awry in your life, your body knows it. And if you bury that knowledge, your body will remind you eventually. Why let the process of revealing, and reconnecting to who you really are, be obscured for longer than necessary?

Most of us know someone who has literally forced themself into a career that paid extremely well but did not use the skills that they valued most. One such friend expressed to me: "I felt my inner soul was literally dying." Eventually, this friend experienced shooting pains emanating from his neck, extending down to the fingers of his left hand. He could not sleep at night. The pain caused by constricted muscles in his neck and his tormented nights pushed him finally into admitting that things were not right. From then on, he was able to explore other directions and make changes.

Your body can indeed deliver powerful messages when your conscious mind tries to repress them. My personal messenger is my skin. Whenever I am not paying sufficient attention to something important, it breaks out in a rash. It covers all the delicate sensitive parts just to make sure I listen and doesn't quit itching till I listen.

The body also responds powerfully to the positive. As you experience love and closeness with your nearest and dearest, as you wander through the extraordinary beauty of nature, feel the exhilaration of diving into a cool lake, even curling up with a beloved pet and a good book, your body responds. Your parasympathetic nervous system is nourished, so you can open and experience the pleasure of the moment.

Often when you find intense delight in a particular moment of presence, your body will reinforce this delight with feelings of softness, warmth, and openness. It is at these times that you can catch a glimpse of the direction you desire. Watch for the feeling of your heart singing. Your truth resides there.

Here are some ways to learn to listen to your body:

a. If possible, once an hour, consciously change what you are doing physically. If you are sitting, stand and walk. If you are active, sit or lie down for a few seconds. As you do so, consciously notice your body and where you feel sensation. As you move or rest, watch what happens to that sensation.

b. When you experience heightened emotional reactions throughout your day, witness them, and take a moment to pause. As you pause, try to identify where in your body the emotion has landed. Hold that place and give it your attention as you direct some deep breath to soothe or enjoy it. When you experience a surge of energy or inspiration, or feel a rush of motivation, notice where in your body it starts. For me and many people, a definite "Yes" for something starts in the stomach and is therefore known as a "gut feeling".

The important question is: once we have started to feel our body "talk" to us, what do we do with that? How do we allow the buried emotions to rise, and find expression? How do we integrate them, make them whole, heal them and learn from them? Only when this happens can they help us know ourselves, know what we want, and reveal the way ahead.

It may be challenging to actually feel emotions that have been buried. It may be necessary to tread very gently and slowly through this process, integrating only as much as you can digest at any one time. For some, it may be too painful, and they may decide to seek help. For others, it will be an altogether freeing, inspiring, and exciting process.

We all have painful memories, failures, disappointments, loss, or shame hidden away or suppressed in our Body Minds. We have the choice to retrieve them, reform and release them. Or ignore them, allow them to fester, and never heal. John Upledger described these repressed feelings as a:

"somato-emotional cyst, a primitive body defense response in which the injury and the emotions therein encoded, are walled off from the rest of the body, and never truly resolve".

Somato-Emotional Release: Deciphering the Language of Life. John Upledger.

There are many ways to release emotion and there is certainly something that works for each one of us. Yoga is my chosen practice. Through Yoga I frequently experience the sensation of unlocking emotion very directly. I feel as if a tender spot in my body, when stretched and squeezed, will release emotion, and allow it to flow to the surface for me to experience fully.

Immediately after my mother's death I was surprised that tears did not flow. I was unable to feel grief. Weeks later, as I bent deeply forward in my yoga practice, my heart finally opened. It no longer had to be upright and strong, it could relax towards the earth with me curled round it and the tears started to splash on the floor. I had unlocked the grief that was buried deep in my heart and the floodgates burst.

Others can release through meditation, breath, hiking, climbing, music, Tai Chi and many other activities.

If you regularly bury or deny your authentic reaction to the world, it is only buried, not banished. It will, in the end, re-emerge as either a physical or a psychological ailment or a wall of protective defense. How can you open to the new, the unknown if you are cowering behind a wall that stops you feeling your feelings, that keeps you safe, but small?

The good news is that as you create space where emotion was once trapped, there is the possibility of new ideas and feelings inhabiting that space. Gradually, as you move into that space, resistance melts away and you can consider a more expansive range of possibilities.

Increasingly, neuroscientists are acknowledging what they call "neuroplasticity" or the capacity of the brain to create new neural connections and grow new neurons in response to thoughts and experience

"When we consider the mind as an embodied relational process that regulates the flow of energy and information, we come to realize that we can actually use the mind to change the brain".

Buddha's Brain. Rick Hanson PhD.

What a concept! If you can get clear enough in the mind/body, you may actually change the physiology of your brain. Nothing is fixed or static, certainly not who you believe you are.

It seems that the more you expand awareness of your possibilities, the more your life may unfold in ways you had previously not even considered. Even the structure of your brain can change to accommodate your evolution.

To summarize, these are the ways your Witness, your ability to be Present and your Body Awareness will prepare you to proceed through this book and life:

- The Witness brings awareness to the endless flow of thought and feeling that passes through you. It helps you "name and tame" overwhelming emotion and helps you transform defensive reactions into authentic responses.
- Presence sets you free to experience life to the full as it happens.
- Physical Awareness helps you to feel emotion as it lands in the body, and release it if necessary, to create space for creativity.

Chapter 2 - *The Big Picture*

Using these practices, we start now to explore your relationship with yourself, with your life, and with money.

I have divided this section into 3 parts:

- First, we bring front and center the fact that life is short; whatever your reality, it is finite and precious.
- Then we look at how intimately you feel a sense of self, a sense of your essence.
- Finally, we inquire in-depth into the quality of your current reality and the role money plays in it.

Life is Short!

"It is a truly cosmic paradox that one of the best teachers in all of life turns out to be death."

The Untethered Soul. Michael A. Singer

The reason I start with this quote is to highlight the importance of having a visceral awareness of the impermanence of life. If you really are serious about not "shuffling" through life, then feeling its impermanence is essential. It is often the case, when someone has a near-death experience, or when a person they love dies, that their appreciation for their own life increases exponentially. It takes a tragedy, sometimes, for people to grasp the frailty of life. How wonderful to have that appreciation without a tragedy.

And once we appreciate the preciousness of life, then it becomes yet more urgent to not waste it, to take its passage very seriously. Maybe we'll die in a week, a year, a decade or two or three, but soon. There really is no time to waste.

For me, the realization of "eternity" occurred at the tender age of seven!

This is how it happened.

My parents were out for the evening, leaving me with a babysitter. It turned out to be the night I first contemplated the finality of death.

The babysitter crept into my bedroom to find a totally hysterical child, terrified of dying.

"Don't worry dear, you may come back as a worm", she counseled.

Oh, the relief! Finally, a concept I could grasp: life after death. Maybe only worm life, but I took it. I could imagine the sweet slimy pinkness of my new form. I could not imagine not being.

On that memorable night I came face to face for the first time with the concept of Eternity, with the idea that one day I would no longer exist, forever. The idea of not being and not knowing what not being would be and worse still, not knowing if there would be anything to not know that I didn't not know, was excruciating!

Luckily the babysitter was a wise woman who knew that this crazed 7-year-old mind was trying to grasp the edges of existential "not beingness" and she knew the idea of being a worm would calm my panic. I settled for the worm and went to sleep. (Secretly embracing the possibility of a princess of course.)

That night I got it! I would die and I didn't know when. And I would be dead forever.

That night I determined to pay very close attention to life as it unfolded, and to what would make it worthwhile. As I grew, I sometimes focused on building security and financial sufficiency. I set about trying to put things "in order", looking for great jobs with good salaries, finding places to live that were good investments, saving for retirement, and generally taking care of business.

Sometimes this worked as planned; when I had built the security I craved, I felt safe, for a while.

Then just when I thought I had everything as it should be, unpredictably a dark hole would descend on my soul. Everything seemed pointless, not the worthwhile life I craved at all. I realized that no amount of safety was going to fill the hollow, and I started to wonder if the quest for security was in fact, part of the problem itself.

So, I switched gears and started "following my passion". Come what may, I threw caution to the wind, desiring only inspiration, adventure, anything to plug the hole of emptiness.

All well and good... until the bills started piling up and I lay awake at night running the numbers, endlessly trying to figure ways to cut back or create money from devious schemes, that did not involve the need to "sell my soul".

It became achingly clear that passion soon waned when accompanied by grinding insecurity!

But what was even more curious was that on the rare occasions when *everything* finally seemed to be lined up: money, passion, health, relationships, etc. even then, low and behold, the gaping hole could *still* sometimes reappear!

Even then, it felt that if I were to die the following day, I did not feel I had yet lived "a worthwhile life".

Where are you on this journey between security and meaning? Have you created a happy marriage between the two? Are you sometimes aware of a gaping hole where your soul should be? Even though everything is lined up and in place.

Increasingly it became clear to me that in fact there was a whole other layer to contemplate. There was other work to be done. After a few decades on this planet, certain parts of me seemed to be withering, and only occasionally did I catch a glimpse of feeling, fleetingly, whole.

No amount of money or security, no amount of excitement or passion, no amount of doing good deeds, automatically led to a feeling of wholeness. I saw that even if I had it all in spades, the hole could appear. This brings us to:

Your sense of Self

I became less and less sure of what exactly was missing. There were no words to define it. Just a vague sense of yearning, of feeling there must be more.

Quite simply my spark was gone, and I felt I had exhausted my options.

What was missing, I eventually realized, was a sense of self, a sense of Me, that would be there no matter how the details of life unfolded. This was essential for it to be MY life that unfolded.

I finally understood that no amount of rearrangement of life's minutiae would create the shift I needed until I re-found my core. Only from that foundation would I be able to navigate the twists and turns that life presents. Only then would I be able to make authentic choices that would help me find what was uniquely worthwhile for me. And paradoxically, only then would I be able to feel peace in my soul even when the circumstances of life were awry!

"We realize that what we are seeking is an intimate relationship with the potent and paradoxically unknowable animating force that stands behind our own creation."

Bringing Yoga to Life. Donna Farhi

And so began the journey home to that animating force. Not to "know" it, but to be it. Not to find words to describe it, just to feel wholly at home in my being.

The great mystic Osho told his students:

Who am I? is not really a question because it has no answer. It is a device, not a question. We can use it like a mantra. The mind will supply many answers, yet we must reject them all. As long as it remains a verbal question, a verbal answer from the head will be supplied. Eventually, we can drop the verbal question. It can remain just a vague idea. When we are not asking it in language and just the feeling of the question is settling in our center, then there is no need for any answer. It is not the business of the mind. The mind will not hear that which is nonverbal, and the mind will not answer that which is nonverbal. Instead, we will get the feel, the taste, the perfume. Then at some point a miracle happens...the question disappears. The question has no more props to support it, so it just collapses. We drop into the Presence that we are.

All you need is to notice, to be present and aware of your physical being.

It is by using the Witness to *notice* whatever moves through you, that eventually you are able to *feel* your animating force and dwell in it.

It is by dropping into Presence that you are actually *there* as you touch the essence of your being and find joy at its core.

It is by becoming aware of your body, whether it is shrinking and cowering, or expanding and dancing, that you can live in your animating force.

Once you feel "settled in your center" and no longer need to ask: "Who am I?", then you can address some of the other big questions and move towards a life that is worthwhile for you:

"Why am I here?" and

"Where am I going?"

As with "Who am I", you don't need to find "the right answer" to those questions, just hold them constantly as background awareness. Hold these questions as you consider the questions later in this chapter. Hold them as you look deeply at how your days pass, how you feel about your days, how much joy you find there.

You will start moving forward more openly, more freely, with more curiosity and less resistance, towards whatever wants and needs to show up next.

Before you start the exercises that follow it is useful to understand how you can become disconnected from your core, how your anima can become dulled.

How is it possible that sometimes we seem to morph into someone we hardly recognize?

There are obviously many factors at play, many ways that life's events can cause us to shut down, to build an intricate system of defense to keep us safe. These defenses may keep us safe, but the price we pay is a gradual separation from our original whole self.

Verbal negativity, perceived failures, criticism, there are so many influences that can push us away from a course we once desired.

Money is surely one of the principal factors for becoming disconnected from your authentic self and pushed from your true path.

How can we possibly ignore the huge power that money has for us as we face each decision and each transition life presents? The very push/pull between "money" and "meaning", between inspiration and security is a powerful determiner of how our life unfolds and how we unfold (or not). We struggle to reconcile security with dreams, we flip-flop between the two, we compromise and even sell our souls. And along the way often, we simply lose ourselves.

Luckily, as a strong sense of self emerges, you are better able to embrace each transition with a full heart and with your need for security honored.

As I began to notice (witness) what was happening when I thought or felt something about money or my future, I was soon able to recognize 5 seemingly contradictory personal truths:

1. The pursuit of money for its own sake could keep me from the life I craved.
2. The pursuit of money could even separate me from my whole self.
3. Money played an essential role in creating the life I craved.
4. Financial security was essential for my well-being.
5. None of the above mattered if my heart was not singing!

Later, when I became a Financial Planner, I learned that I was not alone with these contradictions. I relished the opportunity to help others through this seeming conflict.

Starting with self-inquiry, with Witnessing thoughts and emotions, the conflict starts to dissipate. Money and passion no longer sit on opposite sides of the desk. They unite, become friends, and work together to create lives. This union nurtures our sense of self, allowing it to flourish. How is this possible if you are stuck in a life you hate? Sometimes it requires making a change.

As self-knowledge deepens, not only do Money and Passion become interdependent but their unity becomes an integral part of your self-discovery. You learn not to look at them as a choice, one or the other, but that both coexist in everything you do. The work is to design your own pattern with both, which will be unique to you alone. The balance of financial security and meaning are intimately enmeshed with identity. It takes time and honesty to unravel the entanglement of the two and allow the relationship to evolve healthily and creatively. When you understand this unique dance and understand that if the dance is harmonious, you can sink into a delightful sense of being who you are, create the life that was meant for you, and have the financial base you need.

Life becomes a delightful smorgasbord of opportunity! As Jacob Needleman puts it:

"Any serious search for self-knowledge and self-development requires that we study the meaning that money actually has for us".

Money and the Meaning of Life. Jacob Needleman

Financial security that calms your need for security, is essential.

A life that expresses your true self and potential, is essential.

By first reconnecting with yourself, and then exploring creative options, both are possible.

Feeling fulfilled and feeling secure are not mutually exclusive.

You cannot settle for security if it means losing your soul; if it means a life devoid of joy, exhilaration, zest, anima. You cannot settle for years of being who you are not.

And you cannot settle for financial insecurity. No amount of inspiration will compensate for crawling into bed at night riddled with anxiety about money.

You can have both the financial security you need and a life that is precisely right for you. It is already waiting for you. But first, you must find yourself... just by watching.

Your current reality

Do you know deep in your soul that a shift must happen, but you can't quite define the nature of that shift?

Are you just getting through life, treading water, surviving, waiting, stuck in a rut, stuck at crossroads, putting off the decision of which path to take?

Or are you in love with your life? Do you leap out of bed each morning eager to start the day? Do your days allow you to use the skills and qualities you have that you most value? Do your days allow for the fullest expression of who you are? Do you recognize yourself in others' eyes when they see you, or are they seeing someone else? Are you living the life you thought you would live before it started making demands on you?

Do you know deep in your soul that a shift must happen, but you can't quite define the nature of the shift?

Do you know what makes your heart sing?

What role does money play in all this?

Following are exercises that will illuminate the quality of your day-to-day life.

They will guide you to an awareness of who you are when you are simply being, not doing or interacting. They will illuminate how you are as you move through the details of the life you currently inhabit.

Is this your life? How does it fit? Is it fine just as it is? Does it need a tiny adjustment, or maybe a mammoth shift?

As you move through the experiences and questions on these pages it will always be from the perspective of returning home to yourself.

The practice of watching is fundamental. Allow your Witness to lead home, to that sweet sense of intimacy with yourself.

Take this opportunity to step back from it all and look at what's good, what's lacking, both from an emotional and circumstantial standpoint.

We'll start by tracing your journey thus far. Then we'll consider your relationship to Time, your emotional fluctuations, and your physical condition. We'll look at how you greet each day, what is to be learned from moments of anger and happiness, how you react to new opportunities, "busyness", and regret.

Answer each question with introspection, honesty, and with the intention of learning a little more about yourself and your current situation.

Start now: which is harder for you? Figuring out your financial comfort zone or figuring out your purpose? Which do you enjoy most? Which do you try to avoid? Why? Be curious about everything that arises.

Exercises:

Your Life Map

A Life Map is a list of pivotal moments that either caused a significant change in your direction, or at least an awareness that you had moved into a place of transition. They may be an actual event such as a conversation, or simply a realization that from that time on, nothing would ever be quite the same again.

- Make a list of the major turning points in your life.
- Describe your process and identify the reasons for the decisions you made.

Trace back as far as you can. Some may be dramatic tipping points when you literally hit the wall and made a momentous change, like choosing a university or accepting a job. Others may be longer periods of time when you gradually became aware of a nagging idea that simply would not let you go.

It's important to note anything in your journey so far that seems to have significantly influenced who you have become. As you write, describe the nature of those periods as fully as possible, and inquire deeply into your feelings at the time. You will find everything from feelings of disconnection and flatness to exuberance.

Allow a period of several days, even weeks to complete your Map. It's not the actual writing of the Map that takes time, but the allowing of it all to slide back into your consciousness. We will return to this map several times to view it from different perspectives, so there will always be time to add to it.

When you are finished, leave it for a few days, then return to review it. For our purposes in this chapter the inquiry will be specifically about your process of dealing with these periods of transition.

How did you become aware of them? How did you respond to them?

Becoming aware of how you have reacted in the past to transitions will provide insight into how you have arrived at this point in your life.

- Have you been a victim of circumstance, believing that you had no control, no influence over the decisions, just falling into whatever came along?
- Did you leap impulsively towards each inspiring option?
- Did you grasp at solutions because the unknown was too uncomfortable?
- Have you followed the lead of others or been the leader?
- Were you blown by the wind, whisked through life without much introspection?
- Did you make decisions because of what was expected of you? You didn't want to upset or disappoint others? Was it more comfortable to keep everyone happy?
- Were you drawn to solutions as a result of flattery, being told you would be "perfect" for something?
- Were you drawn towards the safest option, seeking security, financial or emotional?
- To what extent did you make decisions based on fear of the unknown and take the familiar option?
- Do you make decisions based on your "gut" feeling?
- Do you make pro/con lists and calculate every detail?

It is likely that money has played a part in at least some of the big life transitions you have faced. As you trace your journey look both at emotional reasons for your decisions and the part money played. Explore your patterns, expand on the suggestions above.

How have these decisions molded who you are? Are you the sum of all these decisions you have made? Who were you before you made those decisions? Would you be the same person if you had made other choices? Is there still more to you, waiting? Has your evolution through the decisions and chapters been authentic, or were you blown off your course?

Your relationship to time

Now we will look at your attitude to the minutes as they tick inexorably away.

I make a point of asking people in stores, banks, businesses etc. how they are doing. All too often, I hear the following responses:

"TGIF...thank Goodness it's Friday."

"Nearly quitting time."

"Today's great, it's my Friday!"

"Slow day. Time is really dragging today".

And this was the response from a client that I had asked when she hoped to retire. She had the answer dialed into her watch and checked regularly.

"Ten years, eight months, three weeks, twenty-nine minutes"

Are you wishing away precious moments of *your* life? Or do you wish you had more time each day? Does it vary? Our relationship to Time is our relationship to Life Itself. How is your relationship?

In which time frame do you feel most comfortable? Do you reminisce about the past or leap forward into future planning? Are you able to stay present?

Do you wish Time away, watch the clock, live for lunch-hour, Friday, the next vacation, when the kids are in school, when you can retire? Notice this in others as you inquire:

"How's it going?"

"Good day, it's going really fast!"

I've certainly done my share of wishing time (my life) to go quickly. Imprisoned in a classroom with 30 highly challenged adolescents, I finally assigned some mindless "busy" work to keep them occupied while I sat watching each agonized minute tick by. I knew I did not have what it took for *that* challenge and knew I would not be spending the next 30 years willing Time to pass.

How often do you wish *your* life away? Long for the next thing so whatever is happening will be over? One day, it could be tomorrow, it will be over, too late to say: "Hang on a minute, I forgot to live my life!".

- For one week notice throughout each day when and how you react specifically to time. At the end of the day record this information so at the end of the week you will have an idea of whether you are wishing your life away. Are you hungry for more of it, or did you wish your time was spent differently? Just a couple of words daily is enough.

Notice your changing emotions

The quality of your life can be brought sharply into focus by learning to pay close attention to your fluctuating emotions.

By using your Witness, start to notice as your emotions change throughout the day, from exuberance to desperation and everything in between. Which feelings visit most frequently? How long do they last? What causes them? Do they have a pattern? What can they tell you about who you are? Observe the quality of your emotional state when you feel fully alive and when you feel flat, deadened. What happened to ignite each of those emotional reactions?

Watching our emotional state opens the possibility of change. For example, you notice feeling irritated or annoyed whenever things don't go the way you feel they should. The result of this reaction could be that you withdraw and no longer participate. If you notice such a reaction as a pattern, you can inquire into why exactly it is so important to you to have your way, regardless of the desires of others. Tracing its origin may help you "name it and tame it", until it dissipates allowing you to be more flexible and open to alternatives other than those you were fixated on. Dormant sides of you will reawaken.

As you move through your days, notice the fluctuations of your emotions. What precedes each emotional shift? What initiates it? Take a moment to be alone with your feelings, particularly if they are powerful, and trace their origin. Close your eyes and sink into the emotion. Name it. Even say out loud: "Oh, so now you're feeling ……". If the feeling is very familiar, be especially curious about where it came from. Give it attention. And, if it is painful, remember that all feelings are transitory. It will pass.

Even while feeling low, a part of you can rejoice in the anticipation that you may learn something you need to know. But only if you look at it full on and feel it fully. Acknowledge the feelings without judging them and with the knowledge that they are just passing through. What are they telling you?

When you are practiced at watching your emotions, start to distill the messages.

Notice anything that recurs, anything that seems important and record it. As this becomes a regular practice, you may notice recurring themes, and patterns. Periodically read back through your notes and see if something is trying to make itself heard.

The more you learn to watch, the more you reveal about yourself. Each powerful emotion is a potential new source of insight. What you learn from this will gradually become part of your new reality. You will have the possibility to transform back to who you were before "life" started pushing you out of shape! Notice particularly if the origin of the emotions has anything remotely to do with money. Notice also if it has anything to do with a dream or plan you hold dearly.

Observe physical messages

You cannot build a complete picture of your current reality without paying close attention to your physical being.

There is a reason our language includes such imagery as "gut-wrenching", "heartbroken", "gut reaction" etc.

Essentially our mind, body, and brain operate as one, interrelated and interdependent. When abandoned by a lover we feel a deep hollow ache in our chest. When enduring some torturous ordeal our innards literally feel as if they are being wrenched!

Often the child who complains of tummy ache before school when there is nothing physically wrong, is experiencing stress.

Perhaps the woman who constantly complains and worries about ailments is simply screaming for attention.

Even if the mind itself can avoid pain by using excuses, defenses or denial, the body is less subtle. It literally screams at us with aches and pains, rashes, or fatigue if there is something that needs attention. The body can indeed be our best teacher. Your body will tell you a lot about the rest of you if you notice it. And releasing emotion stored deep in the body will bring your truth front and center. The body holds the key to many an unopened door, many a buried emotion.

Lie on the floor with your eyes shut. Relax as deeply as you can. Scan your body and notice how it feels from head to toe. Notice any places that feel tight, ache, itch, are hot, cold, sweaty. Notice pain or discomfort. Place your hands on those places and as you breathe deeply, allow them to soften. Notice if those places change during the day and record in your notebook what you discover about your physical being. Notice as the day passes how things change.

Whenever you are challenged by powerful emotions, notice where they land in your body. Notice the broken heart, the wrenched guts, the gut reaction. Notice the sinking feeling, the jitters, the sweaty palms, the adrenalin rush, the endorphin release. Notice when you shut tight and when you open freely. Notice wherever your body is reacting to what is happening and try to breathe a little deeper with that place in mind.

If possible, treat yourself to a "restorative" yoga class. These are classes where the intention is to relax and renew. The poses are all supported and relaxing and held long enough for your body to release tension and stress. They provide time and space to deeply explore throughout your body, to become more aware of your body and even sometimes to release deeply buried emotions.

Consider taking up a regular Yoga practice if you don't have one already. You may gradually notice both physical and emotional tightness releasing as you start to move deeply into the body. Through twisting and extending, squeezing, and releasing, trauma that has been stored and built over time will let go. The space you create will be available for new opportunities.

Good morning!

The vulnerability of our waking moments is a precious time in which we can often catch a glimpse of how things are. The gems that lie beneath the surface often arise as we emerge from sleep. Allow your Witness to notice these moments.

Make sure you have a pencil and your notebook by your bed. When you go to sleep at night, close your eyes with the intention of noticing your first thoughts when you awaken in the morning.

When you awaken, even before you open your eyes, inquire into the quality of your being: Are you feeling cozy and relaxed with sweet anticipation of the day ahead? Are you aware of your body immediately gearing up to face whichever demands are made first? Try not to judge those feelings or to attach too strongly to them, just take note. The transition from sleep to wakefulness is fascinating when you bring awareness to it. These are moments where there is so much to be learned. If you have been dreaming it is interesting to try and hold the dream, hold its essence, its flavor. Then as the dream fades and reality fills your awakening mind, spend a moment to taste the flavor of that. What are you feeling as you slide into your day?

Pick a few words to describe your emotional being as you awaken. Jot them down before you "think" about them. Do this each day for at least a week, just to see if things change or if there's a pattern. These fluid emotional states are useful teachers in many ways. Notice when you awaken with a sense of dread, boredom, fear, or flatness. Notice when you awaken with a sense of anticipation, excitement, joy and when you awaken with a surge of adrenalin, anxiety. What are the messages of the mornings?

I remember a time when I had just returned from a period of travel and landed back to a home and town that I love. I noticed each morning as I awoke, that although there was delight and anticipation about being home, there was also, surprisingly, a subtle sense of lack. I tried to pay close attention to this feeling despite really wanting to ignore it. I chose to stay with this uneasiness because I knew it held a message I needed to receive. I knew that if I stayed with the discomfort for long enough, something would be revealed.

All this pleasure and I awaken with a sense of lack! Slowly the truth was revealed.

There was a hole where Purpose used to be.

I knew this was my truth and I felt such a sense of relief as I finally had the courage to admit it.

Making excuses

- Out of the frying pan, into the fire...
- Better the devil you know than the devil you don't....
- Don't upset the applecart etc.

Our language is peppered with homilies advising you to "stay safe". Not surprising then that many of us often find excuses not to do something...in order to "stay safe". Use your Witness to heighten your awareness of how often you make an excuse. Use your Witness to honestly question whether you really don't want to do whatever it is, or whether there is some underlying fear preventing you from saying: "Yes!". If you habitually turn away from things that in fact excite you (but maybe frighten you a little), then you risk deadening that excitement entirely and extinguishing a little part of yourself.

Making excuses is the most effective way to lose sight of yourself, your passions, and your dreams.

Notice your habitual response to the myriad of choices and opportunities that life presents. Is your knee-jerk reaction to welcome them with a "Yes!" or make an excuse? Do you retreat with fear or walk towards what might be?

If you choose to close a door, if you choose "No", you supposedly think you have good reasons for doing so, and of course there may be good reasons. Your Witness will help you know whether your reasons are in fact excuses or whether they are authentic.

Sensitize yourself when you hear yourself say things like:

It just doesn't make sense right now.

I can't take that risk.

I'm not well enough to do that.

I don't have a choice.

I have commitments.

I can't afford that.

What about the family?

What about school/college/job?

I'm too old/young.

I don't have the skills/knowledge.

I don't have the strength.

What will people say?

I might fail.

I don't have time.

Maybe later.

Etc.

There are often creative ways to move beyond these objections. You can re-frame the concerns. For example:

"I'm way too old for that" can become "I'd better do it now; I won't be any younger next year".

"I'm not fit enough" can become "If I start exercising, I will get fitter".

"I don't have time" can become "I'll look at how I really use my time now".

"I'll do it later" can become "I'll start planning now".

"I can't afford it" can become "I'll take a good look at how I spend my money".

You nearly always have some choice in how you respond to what life presents. The danger is that if you don't notice and question your automatic response, your way of responding may become habitual until eventually you get so lost in the habit of safety, that you forget what even really inspires you.

Most of us must spend some amount of our lives "taking care of business" and for some this may involve doing things that are not our dream. The challenge is to keep our eyes on the dream, not get lost in "the daily grind" to such an extent that we stop even dreaming our dream. If dreams and inspiration fade, we either morph into someone we are not, or get sick.

The exercise that follows will require you to look honestly at those times when you make excuses. This is challenging because when you make an excuse not to do something that you really, deep down, do want to do, you are denying your desires. You are, instead, responding to the fears that you think will keep you safe. You are stepping away from what you really want, away from coming fully alive again. Looking at fear is uncomfortable.

What are you denying? What are you frightened to say "Yes" to? What are you pretending is OK when really, it's not? What are you putting off? What are you waiting for? When do you not tell the whole truth about what you really want? This is the time to look. Even if you don't act as a result of what you see, you will at least have acknowledged the truth to yourself. Then little by little you can start laying the groundwork for the change that may be coming later...

- Keep a note of each time you choose not to tell the whole truth about what you want, and can't even admit it, even to yourself.

- Notice each time you make an excuse. Notice your habitual response to suggestions and new possibilities. Keep a record of what you are saying "No" to and of the excuses you made.

As you do this work you will lift the mask of denial and excuses and open to the possibilities that could bring you home to your life.

"I'll be happy when…"

A few little words that can be just that - or can be very revealing. It's interesting to watch how often you say them.

On one level it can mean that you have forgotten temporarily to tune into the joy that is always there, waiting to be felt! Take cleaning toilets for example!

"I'll be happy when I've finished cleaning these toilets!".

If I can catch my complaint, then I can instead choose to tune in to how happy I am to even have toilets, and how grateful I am to be physically able to clean them, and to remember that I don't have to clean toilets all day, every day! Not to mention the sheer delight of feeling the air as it passes through my body and the feel of my clothes against my skin, the taste of my tea lingering in my mouth. Then soon I can connect back to being "happy" even when the present moment presents me with a toilet to clean!

But on another level, if those words keep popping up with frequent regularity, they can be yet another subtle messenger that something needs your attention. When is "when" going to be? How long will you wait? What is it that's not allowing you to feel happy right now? Pay attention when you say, "I'll be happy when..." Consider whether it's just because you forgot to notice how happy you are in this moment. Or if something really needs to shift.

- Take note every time you say: "I'll be happy when" and notice what it is that you are doing in that moment that caused you to wish it were different.

Being busy, habitually.

Are you constantly rushed with never enough time to really enjoy any of it? Why is that? Is there too much going on? Are there some things that aren't essential? Are you busy being busy? What fills your time, really? Could you create more time?

Life is demanding, it takes a lot to earn a living, maintain a home, raise children, have fun, keep fit, be social and on and on. But being busy can also be a wonderful drug to hide behind. I am not often alone but I notice that when I am, I scurry around being so busy to avoid my loneliness, to avoid feeling lonely. Avoid feeling. Once I had to clean all the windows, scrub all the floors, change the beds, and weed the garden before I stopped, to feel. I certainly got a lot done but it was frantic avoidance, not delight.

Notice when you are making busy-work. I know this will sound crazy to everyone who really is so very busy with jobs, children, etc. But sometimes those are the periods of our lives when busyness can ubiquitously become a habit. We really get so used to being busy that even 5 minutes with nothing but a void, is unacceptable. And we rush to fill the space. Often with a distraction, a screen, the news, the phone, check messages, check the "market". And we just lost 5 minutes that could have been spacious and reflective. Being distracted is a useful habit to watch.

Over a lifetime, activities that initially seemed necessary to keep things running, can morph into an endless stream of habitual tasks that we forget to question. Routine becomes mindless, habitual, even when it is in fact no longer necessary. In order to live more consciously we need space, time to *be*...not do.

Look at everything you do habitually and question it. Take, for example, that first cup of coffee (or whatever) each day. Did you have one today? Did you taste it? Did you love it? Try just drinking water or juice for a few days and having coffee later. How could you use those minutes it usually takes to make the coffee? Notice the habits that automatically fill each moment, moments that could have been empty, and then try to resist the urge to fill them and just sit and breathe for a couple of minutes. Breathe and relax and notice how the rest of the day changes its tone.

Eventually insert interludes of nothingness throughout the day. Stop, just stop. It is possible to breathe, relax, notice and check in. Pay attention to what is happening and how you feel about it at the moment. Dare to stop. Then ask yourself what you need.

Regret. What do you regret doing/not doing?

As you look closely at the nature of your existence both now and going forward, it is insightful to reflect on what you regret *not* having done.

What were the reasons behind not doing it? What part did money play in that process?

First of all, take a moment to travel back through the chapters of your life and uncover decisions, relationships, periods of time you *do* regret. Things that you now see were clearly the wrong fit for you.

Try to remember how you felt during those times and what it was that led you in the wrong direction. Take note of the times when you were, for whatever reason, off track. Consider not only things that you did, maybe a wrong job or college course but also the way you were as a person at that time. What can you learn about yourself from these periods?

- Write down a few examples of times and decisions you regret. Note what it was about the way you were in the world, that you regret. Note also the qualities that you love about yourself that were, during that time, hidden.
- Now, equally if not more important, think about what you regret NOT doing or being? Catch yourself when you think or say: "I really wish I had……." What opportunities did you not take? Is it too late? Are those ideas still lying dormant within you?
- Notice when you say or think: "If only I'd studied x at college. If only I'd accepted that job. If only I'd

moved to x when I had the chance." Notice if those thoughts are still with you after a couple of days. Notice if you recognize some part of yourself that still needs recognition.

The Tipping Point

A Tipping Point is a moment in time when change happens. It is a moment when a shift occurs that is so powerful that there is no turning back. It is a moment of "knowing", a moment when you can no longer deny your truth.

After this extensive inquiry you may have a better idea of the quality of your life right now, the underlying feel and sense of it, some awareness of what is working and what, possibly, isn't working so well. What words would you use to describe your present existence if you picked just a few?

My hope is that you have begun to understand what it is to feel the spark of what makes you who you are. I hope it has given you some tools to assess the extent your current reality ignites that spark. Does the life you inhabit allow you to be who you are? Or not?

A Tipping Point happens when a message that has been building deep inside you becomes so loud and persistent that it can no longer be ignored. The moment when the "point tips" is unpredictable, and may seemingly come "out of the blue" but when it arrives, you know something will change.

If you are watching closely enough there is a chance to make changes proactively, gently, one step at a time.

Have you ever reached a Tipping Point? Can you recall what triggered it?

Are you nearing one now? Hopefully this work will enable you to see it coming.

A powerful Tipping Point for me occurred as the result of a seemingly innocent comment:

"Your problem is, you have no passion!"

I collapsed internally. Only the Truth could hit me so hard. Somehow, I had arrived in my fourth decade with little sense of direction or passion. Fully aware of the brevity of life, I was treading water. I was not OK with treading water. I knew there was more, and I desperately wanted more.

And although the words had not been spoken maliciously, they touched a deep raw spot. My emotional reaction was so powerful I could no longer turn from this truth.

I had allowed the demands of a "busy" life to swallow me up.

"Your problem is, you have no Passion," was just the kick to the stomach I needed to wake up from this inertia. My strong reaction told me I had to pay attention.

But at first, no matter how hard I paid attention all I could see was a void. At first I was terrified, not jubilant. I was unable even to recognize a passion I had once known. I no longer experienced the rush of energy or pure delight. I remembered those feelings well from before, even as a child, running, dancing, leaping my way through life, laughing uncontrollably, creating, climbing, connecting. Being me.

But suddenly *I* was lost.

Those few words of judgement were my Tipping Point, and I committed in that moment to come alive again.

Tipping Points can creep up on us for a variety of reasons:

- A situation no longer provides further room for expansion and growth without something (or someone) collapsing. Frustration may start to build as our creativity no longer has expression.
- Other times situations are simply a bad fit, or we've outgrown them, or they stop inspiring us. A sense of ennui sets in.
- A situation that doesn't fit with our core values, becomes intolerable.
- A situation that doesn't allow us to express the skills and qualities we value most in ourselves, becomes intolerable.
- A situation simply no longer allows us to live the life we thought we were signing up for.
- Malaise may begin to take hold, and unless you take time to notice, it will eventually consume you.

At some point you will be done with making excuses, feeling envy, hearing yourself say: "I'll be happy when...." and demand: "When IS When?" At some point someone will make a comment that kicks you in the gut, or you'll keep getting aches and pains, sniffles, and rashes. At some point, something, somehow, will remind you of the joyous, exuberant being you are, and your truth will scream for expression. Take as much time as you need to work through this chapter and take as many notes as possible.

Keep revisiting what you have discovered. Read back through your notes repeatedly, add to and adjust them as things evolve. Gradually, the more you watch, the more you are Present, the more you listen to your body, the more your Truth will start to shine.

Gradually, the idea of honoring this Truth will start to feel exciting and energizing even if, at this stage, you have no idea what form it will take.

Embrace the sparks...

Chapter 3 - *Rekindle Life-Force*

"A grand adventure is about to begin."
Winnie the Pooh. A.A. Milne

It's time to inquire into what really does bring you alive – to rediscover what it is that you long for.

Our fundamental questions will be:

What is it that I want?

What is it that makes my heart sing?

What is the life that I was put here to live?

For now, put aside all financial considerations and allow your soul to fly. Money comes later.

Our culture too often does a great job of putting a lid on our dreams. It feeds us objections and rationalizations until dreams just wither on the vine and our energizing Life Force fades. In this chapter we will unearth those parts of you that have been temporarily submerged. We will explore what you yearn for, in order to rekindle your Life Force. We will unearth your passions and desires to reveal your way forward.

Life Force is the spirit or energy that animates every living creature. Each person's Life Force is completely unique to them and is aroused in ways that are different from every other soul. We see Life Force in every baby, as they chortle, giggle or gurgle through their days. We see the absolute delight (or disgust) that fills them for no observable reason.

Life-force can be felt as a surge of motivating energy deep within you when your attention is ignited and drawn like a magnet. Unfortunately, during a lifespan this animation can become dulled or even lost and need to be brought back to life!

So, let's consider here the unique nature of your Life Force, let's discover **where** it is to be found, and **how** you can feel it surge.

The second half of the chapter provides a set of exercises to help you on this quest.

As you proceed through this chapter recognizing passion, feeling attraction, and rekindling energy, you may come to realize that change of some sort is imminent. This may result in feelings of fear, apprehension, doubt, even panic. I will suggest ways to prepare for, and hopefully preempt this.

There will be little mention of money in this chapter for very specific reasons: first because money is often part of the reason our Life-Force becomes dulled and second because our intention here is to allow our dreams and desires to flourish and expand completely unhindered by monetary concerns.

We look first with a broad lens at some sweeping views of how others have defined their life's purpose. Then, as we proceed we will look only at how to touch *your*s. These generalized thoughts of others may stimulate ideas that have lain dormant for a while.

As you read them watch for your reactions.

"A person's life purpose is nothing more than to rediscover, through the detours of art or love or passionate work, those one or two images in the presence of which his heart first opened."

Albert Camus

"My purpose is to write. Not to be famous, successful, or rich. But because if I don't write I don't feel like me".

Andre Dubus III

"Life is a daring adventure, or it is nothing at all"

Helen Keller

"Engaging in the full range of experience -- living and dying, love and loss -- is what we get to do."

Lucy Kalan

"It is alright to wish yourself well, just like wishing the best for any living being. It is alright to do well according to your nature, going as far as you can in this life down the path of contentment, love, and wisdom. To live in love and peace."

Buddha Brain. Rick Hanson

"Don't ask what the world needs. Ask what makes you come alive and go do it. Because what the world needs is more people who have come alive"

Howard Thurman

"I think that enduring, committed love between a married couple, along with raising children, is the most noble act anyone can aspire to. It is not written about very much."

Nicholas Sparks

Many different ideas. Which of them, or which parts of them, resonate with you?

How would you describe, in a few words, the best expression of your life's purpose? Take a few moments to jot down ideas.

How does your current reality align with what you have written?

Approach all the questions here with curiosity and intrigue, not with judgement and guilt! The intention is not to feel bad about yourself or your life, but to open to possibilities that may be waiting.

Let's start with:

Where to find Life Force?

Where *is* my elusive Life Force sequestered?

Do we look within ourselves to find that spark of energy? Or do we look to stimulus from the "world out there" to bring us fully to life?

The answer is both and both are essential. But try as you may, there is no way you can "think" your way back to your Life Force by having ideas about it! It is no good thinking you are riveted by something. You either are or you aren't!

When you are truly alive, there is no denying it. Your energy is on fire! You are engaged, focused, and complete. And this feeling may arise from deep within you in moments of stillness, or it may arise from delight in the world around you: nature, art, music, ideas, a dear friend, purposeful work.

And the wonderful thing is that the energy behind your Life Force is the same as it has always been. You still are who you were as a newborn! Your heart already knows how to sing! You already *are* what you desire.

But sometimes life-force lies dormant and dulled, you need to lift the veil to release it, unpeel the layers and set it free!

"The quest is not a vertical evolution toward something else or somewhere else but a spiraling involution in which the end marks the beginning".

Bringing Yoga to Life". Donna Fahri

I remember a time when I was specifically struggling to figure out my next step, struggling to reconnect with who I am.

I had left town for a week with the specific intention of "figuring it out". I went armed with notebooks, pads, and pencils to make lists, prioritize, think, and write.

All this was useful as it focused the mind and took me away from other distractions.

But it was not enough.

The insights I caught that week occurred when I least expected them, when I was far from "working" at it. They occurred when I was fully present.

On one occasion I was on a long walk, my surroundings so beautiful they stilled my mind, the movement of my body stilled my mind. As my mind slowed, as it became united with the beauty around me, I became aware of a deep arousal of feeling, of feelings that were undeniably my truth. And my heart sang with love, with knowing. In those moments there were no words to describe what I felt. I simply felt that "me-ness" I have mentioned before, and in that moment, I felt confident that any decisions I made would arise from that core.

So, part of the answer to the location of Life Force is that it lies deep within us where you are the most vulnerable, open and real. It is always ready to be reawakened. Sometimes it's just a question of being still enough, open enough, to notice the force when it surges through you.

But Life Force is awakened not only from within. Our journey inward, our "spiraling involution" remains constant and alive as we interact with the vast array of experiences that life presents.

With a soul that is open and receptive, you will feel perhaps your Life Force surge as you engage with a person, as you recognize something deep in your soul as you gaze at a work of art, you feel your energy engage as you listen to a lecture, as you surf the waves, as you listen to opera, as you solve a problem.

It's as simple as recognizing, with honesty, where you find **yourself** as life unfolds. And where *you* are lost, disconnected.

- Take a moment now to reflect back through your life. Focus on moments where you see your Essence shining. Moments where you truly recognize your self. Deeply feel what it's like to be You. Talk to your partner or a friend about each other's moments.

Rekindle Your Life Force

As always, your tools will be watching, observing, noticing, and recording. Continue to notice, as you move through your days, when your unique spark is ignited.

Using your Witness and staying present, tune in to pleasure as it arises, to joy as it fills you, to fascination when your attention is fully engaged. None of this is possible if your mind is racing forward to what comes next, or analyzing what just happened. How will you notice when your attention is drawn if you are worrying about others' opinions, about your success or failure, about today's work? Your Witness will keep you present, free to receive powerful bursts of inspiration when they inspire you.

How can you feel that inspiration, pleasure, joy, fascination if you are, basically, absent?

And how can you feel the rush of Life-Force if you are not totally honest in your responses to life?

Being authentic as you respond to everything that happens requires a level of honesty that may be quite sensitive to touch. But you will not experience the fire of your Life-force if you are habitually pretending, if you are pleasing others, or doing what you *should* do?

Resist the pressure of going with the consensus, fitting in.

Why do we do that? "Fitting in" protects us from rejection, from failure, criticism, or just the unknown. But it can separate us from things that in fact, excite us. We do things from a sense of obligation or guilt and become distanced from our true responses to life.

Resist the temptation to show enthusiasm just because everyone else is. Resist the push to participate because you feel you should. And notice when you feel interest in something that bores someone else. Stay true to that interest, to what it is that animates you, and hold that sacred.

Stay curious and notice when you are responding on autopilot. Ask: "Is that true? Am I being true to my Life Force?"

Only then can you lift the veil that blurs, unravel the web that restricts and dissolve the defenses and delusions that keep us safe but sequestered.

And remember, fully opening to your Life Force will shape the rest of your life:

"The quality of your consciousness at this moment is what shapes your future".

The New Earth. Eckhart Tolle

Maintain non-Attachment

Once you taste the thrill of Life Force, the feeling of your Self, then it is very tempting to grab the first opportunity for change and speed the journey back to wholeness.

My experience is that this doesn't work. Even though uncomfortable, it's better to be with indecision, ambivalence and wavering so life can unfold gradually without pressure or urgency. Remember, Life Force is not only ignited by external circumstances. Things don't have to be a certain way, all lined up in perfect order. Life force is felt as a gentle smile of recognition, simply by being you. It is felt at any moment of pure presence, even amidst total indecision and confusion.

So, stay flexible, flow with indecision, U-turns, fresh starts, contradictions, ambivalence, wavering and hesitation. They may be a vital part of your process.

Above all, stay open. Once you attach strongly to a perceived solution, the danger is that you close to everything else. You cling and close! Then, if something else shows up, something you had never dreamt of, you may simply reject it out of hand, not give it a second thought. After all, the problem is solved, right?

Stay unattached so things can evolve as they are meant to, unexpectedly. Change will evolve, organically.

Gradually you will find that you stay close to a path that is the fullest expression of who you are, a path that meanders and changes, is sometimes straight and direct, sometimes full of twists and turns, and often imperfect.

Pay Attention to Your Attention

Pay close attention to where your attention lands. The choices are endless.

Approximately 400 billion units of information potentially impact your mind daily, but your brain admits only 2,000 of them. Why do you pay attention to one thing, not another? Why does your brain register one idea, not another?

It is time to slide the wedge of awareness subtly into every moment of your day and observe where your attention falls, which pieces of information attract you. This requires presence. If you are lost in mind chatter or simply unconscious of where your attention falls, you will miss a lot. If the Witness is watching closely, you are more likely to consciously choose what to filter out, what to let in. You may venture into vast realms of unexplored potential.

Our habit is to adhere to patterns that already exist in our brains and filter out the rest. Why do we always let in the same information when as children we absorb new information every day? Why do we keep recreating the same reality, same relationships, and same jobs when there is a whole sea of potential experience out there to consider? How would it be if we expanded the range of stimuli rather than contracting it? Would we find parts of ourselves that currently lie dormant? Or reawaken those that have fallen away, from misuse?

The seed of potential change lies within those moments of focused attention, and this can be unnerving. How much easier (if deadening) to plod along the well-worn path.

So, before we proceed, I want you to consider ways to deal with the fear that may arise as you allow new ideas, new ways of being, new possibilities for change, into your realm of experience.

Here are some ways to quiet the panic that may arise when you open to the possibility that your life may be turned on its head!

Stay calm

As you experience the exercises that follow, I hope that you begin to feel a resurgence of Life-Force, and a sense of your unique essence. I hope you start to reawaken desire, passion, and some clarity about your next chapter in life.

You may start to acknowledge that some element of change is necessary. This may cause you some anxiety and fear as change may threaten your sense of safety, and security, especially as you put it in writing, especially as you name it.

But remember, you cannot deny change if change is required to keep your light shining. And you cannot deny the security you need to stay safe. You have to make peace between both. You have to find a way to make change *and* honor the security you need.

So, don't worry about the specifics of the change at this point. Simply embrace ideas as they happen. Stay open to them all. The more you commit yourself to detail the more frightening it will seem, especially if you are contemplating major changes, and especially if it involves a significant financial upheaval.

If anxiety does center around finances, rest assured that there is always a solution to the obstacles that money presents. And we will be outlining many of these solutions in later chapters. The purpose of money is to *enhance* your creativity, not to thwart it. If you dwell on the financial consequences at this stage, you are at risk of abandoning your plans. You will learn how to marry your plans to a financial solution that fits your financial comfort zone. Remember, it is a*lways* best to avoid taking financial steps that cause you stress.

The body's response to danger is to run away or to fight. We face fear with a flood of hormones that boost the body's heart rate, sending extra blood to the muscles, preparing us to run or fight. Our heart races, we sweat, our breath shortens. This is no way to face important decisions you are trying to make that may affect the rest of your life.

First, you must find a way to calm your nervous system and mind. Take as much time as you need, and if you need to take a break or back off, do so. But don't give up. Set the date for when you will take another look, take the next step.

In the meantime, enlist a team of calming techniques, whatever they are.

There are many options. I choose Yoga and running. For me, both are a meditation, and both bring my attention firmly to my breath, which keeps me centered. Others find long walks soothing, hot baths, an escapist book or movie, music, swimming, a chat with a good friend, whatever it takes to relieve the attacks of doubt.

I'll share with you a technique my friend John developed to stay calm as he started his business.

John had long felt a calling to start his own business, and the nature of his business involved a lot of public speaking, creating a big presence in his community and beyond. John was not an extrovert, and the thought of this exposure terrified him. His greatest fear was "Public Humiliation".

Initially he took only very small steps and gradually he noticed that each step was giving him more muscle. Even so, he was frequently attacked by his Inner Critic, particularly in the dark hours of the night.

When John was sick of the fatigue and paralysis his Inner Critic was inflicting on him, he found a solution. He decided to write it a letter, a kind but firm letter, letting the Critic know who was boss.

The letter started like this:

"I understand that you are trying to keep me safe, and in order to do that, you are advising me not to take risks. I understand that to keep me safe you are trying to keep me small. I appreciate that you are trying to keep me safe, but we're doing it anyway. Otherwise, you'll undermine us, and we'll get nowhere. In order to ensure our success, I'm going to: 1. Get enough rest. 2. Not drink. 3. Clear my calendar so I can focus."

John's business grew. Not every step went smoothly but instead of beating himself up for the perceived failures and jettisoning the whole project, he re-evaluated and wrote the Inner Critic another letter!

This continued until John's business gathered enough momentum for him to believe that things would work out.

As his confidence grew, his business caught on and he is now in high demand. But even as he faces each new challenge, he still writes letters to that nagging voice inside his head telling him how inadequate he is!

So, as you start to open to moments of clarity, watch out for that Inner Critic casting doubt and if necessary, write it a letter. Don't let it sabotage your inspiration even as it germinates. Allow yourself to stay with those moments of realization, moments of knowing. Settle into them and see how they feel. Do they take hold and start to evolve? Does your energy start to flow? Or not?

To sum up...

Here are a series of questions that will help you to see your way forward.

When something resonates, sink into the delight of feeling a part of your Self resurface.

For now, put doubt in a box and ask it to wait.

Allow desire to rise to the surface. Explore new or dormant territory.

You may experience a sense of "involving" toward your essence. You may encounter many sources of inspiration that awaken your animating force. You may experience a leap of joy at something that crosses your path. Eventually you may just notice that life has evolved in unexpected ways without you even making any big decisions or dramatic changes. You may just feel led in a way that feels right.

Once this starts, it will continue for the rest of your life, and your horizons will forever expand. Energy may ebb and flow but returning to self-inquiry will become more and more intriguing and, rewarding.

Exercises:

Carry a notebook specifically for this process and always carry it with you. Inspiration can hit at any time, and you need to make a note of it.

Here are a few suggestions that may help you with the questions:

- Above all leave the question of money on one side. Later we will transform money into an ally, not an excuse. Right now, we will ignore it.
- Remember that there is no goal to reach, no problem to solve, no definitive answers to the questions. The answers will always be changing.
- Stay curious, notice waves of intensity and notice when you feel a charge grabbing your attention. Notice when you feel fully alive. Notice when your heart sings. Approach these inquiries not always with an active mind, but with a still mind.

- Be with each question or set of questions over a period and notice, in moments of presence, what arises.
- Reject nothing. Leave analysis, discernment, and judgment for later.
- This is not to say that what you want will be static. Our interests and desires evolve as we do, changing and flowing. Stay fluid.
- Don't cling to any one direction, attached to it being a certain way. Life surprises us at every turn if we allow it, and often takes quite a different form than we had expected.
- As you explore, try looking at things from many angles.
- Question everything. Ask frequently: "Is that really true?"

Background

In the last chapter we started by reflecting on the big choices we've made and how they have evolved into our current situation.

We will start again with a reflection of the past:

- Which parts of your life are you drawn to, parts that made you feel whole, at ease? Make a list of the periods of your life that felt the best; times you remember that felt as if you were in tune with yourself, when you were being exactly who you wanted to be. What are the qualities of yourself during those periods that you like? What were you doing that allowed you to be that person?

- At what times have you felt incomplete, awkward?
- What is missing from the picture you are creating now? How much of yourself do you recognize in it?
- What would you like to remove? What would you like to expand? What would you like to add?
- This first look can be unsettling. Try to look with an open mind and heart, not grasping onto the good parts, nor pretending the less good parts were some other way, just stepping back and accepting your reality and observing your reactions.

What has triggered your desire to re-assess?

- Have your circumstances changed so that your life has been turned on its head?
- Are you feeling the glimmerings of fidget such that you want to pre-empt a tipping point?
- Have you been presented with a major decision that has brought you to this assessment?
- Are you at a midlife crossroad where you are questioning if you really do want to sign up for the second half being the same as the first?
- Has your financial situation changed?
- Are you overly stressed and need to re-assess?
- Are you losing sleep or getting sick for no apparent reason?
- Is there just a sense of lack, a sense that YOU are somewhat absent?

These are only suggestions to help you get clear about why exactly you are thinking about change. Describe your own reasons.

Having re-traced your history so far in terms of what worked and what didn't and what has finally pushed you to consider a shift, let us turn now to the question:

"What is it that you want?"

This question may be totally daunting so here are some other questions to help identify your starting point:

- Are you looking at a total void? Do you literally have no idea about what comes next, a blank canvas?
- Do you have ideas about which area of your life needs attention, but not specifically what needs attention?
- Do you already have a clear idea about your direction, but you can't quite admit it yet, even to yourself?
- Are you clear about direction but unable to get out of the starting gate?
- Are the details of your plan just too overwhelming?
- Are you clear about direction but paralyzed by fear?
- Is the issue of money too much to contemplate?
- Do the money issues seem insurmountable?

Write down anything you know about what you want, however outlandish, however seemingly unrealistic, however big, or small, especially if you don't know where the idea came from. There is a good possibly it came from a part of you that has lain dormant for a while and is crying out to be heard.

At this point, no-one else has to see what you write, not even your partner. Be as specific as you can about what you think you want, now, and be curious, as you work, to see how things evolve.

What is missing?

In Chapter 2 you began to reveal the overall flavor of your life, to recognize when your heart *does* sing as opposed to merely humming! It is useful at this point to get more specific about what is limiting your Life Force, about the areas of your current existence that are calling for your attention.

As you read my suggestions and feel into your own, try not to sink into this as a purely intellectual exercise. Stay present to your emotions, notice any desire to avoid, notice defensiveness, resistance, irritation. Also stay present to physical reactions, tightness, sweat, cold, even pain.

My ideas below are only suggestions. Allow them to inspire your own.

> *There must be a shift in my work, I'm bored.*
>
> *I need more time to explore xyz...*
>
> *I don't feel my xyz skills have expression.*
>
> *I need more contact with people in my life.*

I need more meaningful purposes in my life.

I feel numbed by routine.

I want to leave the world a better place.

I can't take this level of stress anymore.

I feel as if I am at a crossroads, but I can't see the way forward.

I feel strongly about xyz, I need time to pursue that.

I want more excitement, variety.

I need a big adventure.

It's a problem for me to be inside all the time.

I'm not in tune with the people around me.

I'm out of touch with who I am. How did this happen?

I don't feel appreciated for who I really am.

My soul is screaming to get out.

I crave stillness and quiet.

I just need more time for myself.

The life I am living is not in tune with my deepest held values.

I want to be of value to the world, but I don't know what my value is.

I don't know what I want but I feel an unrequited desire!

Give yourself a few days to get to the core of what you are feeling. This is a starting point that can be revised and revisited as things evolve. Try to define your current truth.

As you see in the example below, the truth can sometimes touch a raw chord but write your first thought about what needs to change. It may look something like this:

"My work does not express my core values. I feel as if I am bending my truth in order to please my superiors, to make money. I feel as if I am prostituting myself to success. I need to change the direction of my work". Or:

"I have just retired, and I feel useless. I need to find my value for the next chapter of my life." Or

"I am so stressed I feel I never ever get caught up and find time to simply BE."

Even if your statement is far less precise than any of these, expressing something you know to be true but that has been buried, may feel risky. This is because once you have committed to something in writing it takes on a different level of credibility and may have repercussions. It may result in you taking action, creating change. And change causes ripples of reaction that may indeed upset the applecart.

"It takes courage to take a risk because we have to confront our greatest fears and limited beliefs about what is possible. But the rewards are great. Taking risks expands our comfort zone by creating different

neural pathways and experiences for us that become our new known. It makes life juicy; we feel more alive"

Twenty Questions for Enlightened Living.   Julia Tindall

Our goal here is that the journey be gentle and rewarding and that the risks are stimulating, not scary. If the alternative to change is stagnation and resignation, then juicy is certainly worth a little risk.

Discover what you want in small ways…,

With screams of outrage, frustration and delight, children make it quite clear that they know what they want!

But as the years pass, the demands of peers, parents, schooling, and the media seem to distance us from this instinctive raw desire. We learn to please others.

Researchers have demonstrated this by asking girls at various ages what kind of pizza topping they want. At age 5 they know exactly what to choose. By age 10 they waiver and start to become indecisive. By age 15 the response when asked is more often: "Oh, it doesn't matter. I'll have what everyone else wants".

Some of us find it easier to accommodate the desires of others before our own. On one level this is a generous and selfless trait. The danger, however, is that over time our own desires start to fade.

You need to practice knowing what you want. You need to remember how it felt to want before you learnt to want what everyone else wants you to want! Remember how it feels when your heart sings out with desire. This doesn't mean being selfish, putting yourself before others, but simply knowing your preference *and* enjoying those of others.

Notice when your reasons involve money.

Practice making decisions that reflect what you genuinely want. Practice getting back in touch with desire.

- Make a note at the end of each day the decisions you have made together with the process that led you to your decision.
- Make a note also concerning the role money played in each of those decisions.

Notice joy

We touched on "happiness" briefly in chapter 2 when noticing how often we say: "I'll be happy when...." Now let's go deeper and find out how it can help your quest for knowing what you want.

Happiness, joy, a sense of quiet contentment, wellbeing, exuberance... some of the many words that describe moments of pleasure and delight.

Often people describe a feeling of wellbeing when they are truly Present, when mind chatter and distraction is at a minimum.

"Transcendence, lightness of being, freedom and happiness are not things that we attain; they are what

we become and are. It is what we have always been and what we always will be."

Bringing Yoga to Life.   Donna Fahri

The trick is to return often to that innate freedom and happiness. Each time you step into a moment of Presence, you find it there!

Much has been written through the ages on the elusive topic of happiness in the quest to pin it down! Recently National Geographic (November 2017) researchers came up with three essential ingredients: Purpose, Pleasure and Pride and certainly when we have purpose, when we enjoy what we do and feel pride in our endeavors, that is a reason to feel happy. But sometimes, as we have already observed, even when life is brimming with purpose, pleasure and pride, there can still be a sense of lack. And conversely there can be great joy when everything is awry!

So, although happiness can indeed result from the details of our life, from what *happens*, the other side of the coin is our ability to touch that flow of wellbeing that exists within us no matter what is happening.

If it's that simple, the question then becomes: "What keeps us from happiness?" Why is there sometimes a veil between us and exuberance, even an impenetrable fog?

There are many reasons, but I will mention just 2 here that are relevant to our purpose.

The first is the voice in your head! The voice that repeats the same script over and over, holding you captive. It's the voice that tells you you're not good enough, or that you're really good, or that you're special, or stupid, hated or loved etc. This voice can really interfere with your sense of well-being as it keeps you striving for approval or clinging to the fragile bliss of success. It has the potential to make you suffer and to keep you from yourself.

Learn to listen to the voice. Sometimes that is enough to quiet it and set you free. Get to know your scripts and decide if they serve you.

Secondly, I believe that money has the power to extinguish the spark and that it is why it is our focus in this book.

Naturally, the basic needs of life must be met: food, shelter, clothing etc. But it seems that too often, the pursuit of money becomes a habit, sometimes even an addiction, an end in itself, and you lose sight of your big picture. Here we hope to redress that balance so that your picture comes back into clear focus and money becomes your tool not your master.

As you lift the veil and reawaken to joy, remember to be discerning. Learn to discriminate between the real thing and the power of approval to make you feel good. Learn to recognize when your ego is enjoying a massage and when joy is unconditional.

Learn to observe happiness; when, how, and why it arises. Moments of joy are an invaluable guide to your way ahead. They are the conduit to your unique, expansive adventure ahead.

Allow Presence to awaken both the joy that you are, and the joy the world offers. Start to move fearlessly towards new experiences, possibilities, and challenges.

- Sit for a while, focused on your breath, allowing the mind to steady and slow until you start to feel how you are at the moment.... physically and emotionally.
- Still sitting quietly, direct your attention to moments throughout your life that fill you full of joy and love. Start right back in childhood and allow the moments when you felt really happy, to bubble up. Revisit them. Where were you? What were you doing? Who (if anyone) were you with? What words would you give specifically to the feeling? Later, take your notebook and list them, adding more as you remember. When did your heart sing?
- Practice sitting with your breath every day, just for 5 minutes. Be curious if you can experience not only what is bubbling in your mind but, as it calms, a simultaneous feeling of delight in that moment of stillness. Notice what bubbles up in your heart.
- During the next week have your awareness open to moments of happiness. Notice when they arise and be very curious. What was the genesis, the source of those moments? Where were you? Who were you with? What were you doing? Were you active or quiet, absorbed in an activity, working, or playing? Make notes. As you write, try to describe specifically how it felt. Did you experience a rush of exuberance, a sense of optimism, satisfaction, delight, peace, pleasure, a sense of purpose, of

pride? Also try to observe where in your body you felt the sensation.
- Notice how your body feels when you are happy. Just take a moment to dwell in the feeling and scan your body to get in touch with how the muscles, joints, organs, how it all feels when you feel joy.

Tune into Passion when you see it in others.

One way to reveal your own passion is to notice it in others.

Passion is infectious!

As you observe it in others, you may start to recognize it in yourself. Maybe you will recognize a grand all-consuming passion, maybe you will feel the rekindling of a buried interest. Maybe you will just recognize in others a feeling of rightness, of people living their "right" lives.

Their enthusiasm shines from every pore of their being, no matter what their path may be. What is it about them that is so contagious?

I experienced it was in a funky little cafe. While taking my order, the cook regaled me with vignettes of his ingredients (Stella the ewe who provided milk for Halumi in a local village), then scurried off to the tiny kitchen to create my food, presenting it, beaming with pride in his accomplishment.

There it was in an art gallery where work spilled from the walls, down the stairs, up the ceilings, into the bathroom. The artist claimed to work till 2 am, each night and his eyes twinkled with energy as he described the evolution of his process.

Allow yourself to be infected by the enthusiasm of others. Reflect on times you have felt the same.

Just listen to a favorite piece of music and allow the musician's soul to touch your own. Allow their passion to ignite your own.

The sources of passion are as varied as the people on this planet, everything from symphonies to grains of dust, from dinosaurs to roofing materials. Some people seem to be born with a powerful passion that forges a single track through life. Others have a variety of interests, eclectic pursuits that thrill them. Whenever we feel drawn, attracted, awakened by something that connects us to our own uniqueness, to the essence of who we are, then we are starting to glimpse a way forward. Watch out for other people who seem to be living the right life for them.

- When you are ready, make a list of people you encounter whose lives are filled with passion. Describe them. Note what qualities they have that let you see their passion.

Notice when YOU feel inspired

What does it mean to feel inspired? To me it means that something draws and stimulates my attention and ignites a desire in me to stay close to it. It motivates me to take action, often creative action. It touches a chord deep within me that I recognize as a part of my soul.

Notice when you feel this strong pull of attraction. Watch for those delicious moments when you feel inexplicably drawn, when your interest is fully alert, when you are delighted, entranced, and fascinated by something, somewhere, someone. Notice when you hope something never ends, notice when at the same time you feel excited yet strangely comfortable "at home", when something is touching and igniting the sense of your own uniqueness.

Notice again how your body feels in these moments. Are the sensations subtly different from feelings of happiness? How are they different? For me, I experience a softening when I feel happy, my muscles, joints everything seems to relax, and the smile that usually appears on my face spreads throughout my whole body. Inspiration, on the other hand, for me brings a sense of urgency, an element of tension. Desire creates a degree of attachment and there can be a level of tightening in my body as I strive to get closer to the object of inspiration, to prolong and expand the experience.

- When you feel ready, start to record times that you feel inspired. Notice how it feels in your mind and body. Name the source of inspiration. Did it inspire you to do anything? Did it excite a sense of desire? Did it help you towards feeling something you want in your life?

Pay attention to strong emotion

Noticing feelings of outrage over perceived injustice can help guide us to where we may feel inspired to direct our attention and energy. Notice feelings of outrage. Notice when you are irritated or triggered and notice what happens in your body at those times.

Do you feel upset when you hear of a colleague being unjustly fired or when you see a mother yelling at a small child? Do you feel outrage when you think about climate change, bulk production of eggs, when you see pesticides being sprayed on crops? Do you suffer when you see malnourished children on the news or when you see the slaughter of war? Do you get upset when you hear of female genital mutilation or child labor, the sex trade, animal experimentation?

What do you really care about?

Maybe none of these issues pushes your button but sooner or later something will.

Notice what triggers you on a personal, political, global, and local level. Notice if you care more about starving children in Nigeria or gang violence in Chicago. Notice if you care more about child prostitution or gun violence. Notice if you care more about wage inequality for women. Notice if you care more about deforestation in Malaysia or the spotted owl in the northwest. Or even that your favorite menu item is not available at a restaurant. Or when your friend is sad or lonely.

- Record what you notice and allow yourself to feel passionately about whatever it might be. I'm not suggesting you will go out and "save the world" or even get involved in any of these issues, but your reactions will teach you about yourself. You will see a pattern as you note them. Be honest, no-one will see your list. If the strongest emotion you feel is

about the color of the neighbor's door, don't judge it. Note it. The purpose here is to discover your true passions and interests and only then will you be able to offer to the world your unique gifts.
- When you have several items on your list, group them and observe what dominates. Do you seem to care more about people, politics, animals, aesthetics?

Envy

Feeling envy can often be tinged with feelings of resentment.

And those very feelings of resentment can sometimes clarify precisely what we yearn for ourselves.

We'll look later at how envy may reveal our way forward but for now, just notice when you feel jealousy. Perhaps you even feel resentment towards someone for what they have, who they are, the very quality of the life they are living. Notice when you meet someone, read about someone or see a TV/film character that arouses feelings such as: "I hate him/her, that is exactly the life I want. It's not fair!" At times like this the healthy option is to turn to gratitude for what you have and allow any resentment and dissatisfaction to fade.

But later, when the negativity has dissipated, it may be useful to revisit the impetus for your envy and to see what you can learn. What was it about the source of your envy that enticed you? What stroke of insight did it provide into your desire? Take a glimpse at what inspires you.

We are taught not to feel jealous. Jealousy makes us feel less than, inadequate and resentful. This feeling can drive a wedge of separation.

But it may also hold rich potential for inspiration. It illuminates what we admire, possibly things we recognize as having once been active in us but that we have, for whatever reason, allowed to wither. This may be painful and cause us to resent those who still shine with those qualities.

If you can notice when envy arises, you can turn it into insight. If you are finding it challenging to see your way forward, celebrate when you see someone else where you might like to be! What a gift. Turn envy into inspiration and be grateful for it.

Even if an idea seems ridiculously out of reach, still notice. At some point in time, you may be surprised to see the kernel of a future idea germinating in a moment of envy months ago.

For now, just notice those feelings, don't push them away as negative and nonproductive, embrace them as informative. Enjoy the thrill they engender. Transform jealousy into learning.

- As you encounter them, make a list of people you admire, lifestyles that intrigue you, occupations that appeal, places that attract you. Instead of resenting others, let them inspire you. What can you learn from your lists? Could you incorporate some of the things you admire into the tapestry you are creating?

- If you could be anyone in the world, who would you choose? Whose life would you like?

Flow days.... they are a metaphor for life.

Even if it is totally unrealistic to shelve obligations at this point in your life, the point of this exercise is to catch a glimpse of who you were before the routines took over, to create space for choices, your creativity, allowing decisions to be spontaneous, true in the moment rather than the result of automatic repetition.

Given the freedom to choose, why would you change course during your day? What makes you stop one thing and start another? Where does that impulse come from? Possibly you look outside, see it's a nice day and feel the desire to go out. Possibly you have been active all morning and feel the need to use your brain. Sometimes an urge just seems to arise. Is it a habit? Is it the way you are wired? Enjoying a flow day will take you into all these questions.

Flow days can reveal lifelong patterns.

- If you are able, set aside a full uninterrupted day with absolutely nothing on your schedule. If a whole day is not possible, try for half a day, or even an hour.

Flow days are days when you have no plans, commitments or obligations. Your intention is to stay present and simply follow your inclinations as they move you.

Check in with yourself when you wake and question everything you do habitually. If you usually fall out of bed and reach for a cup of coffee, stop, wait. Ask yourself if you really want coffee at this moment. Consider other options: a run, a shower, tea, yoga, an hour's reading, a phone call, a bike ride, coffee out? Many options. What do you really want at each moment?

Whatever you decide, do it. Do it until you feel the urge to transition to the next thing. Maybe you'll spend the whole morning reading, running, cooking, chatting, but whatever it is, continue until you feel the need for change. When you do, acknowledge the need for change, acknowledge that at first you may not know what you want next, be in unknowing, be in transition in your day, until the next thing piques your interest. Allow yourself to move towards that, until you just feel tired, and the day ends. Before you sleep, take note. What was in your day? Did you flow easily from one thing to the next? How did you find out what was to come next? How did you feel at the moments of transition? Did you find yourself longing for routine, your habitual activities, was the blank canvas challenging? How did you decide what was to come next?

Did you find the pull towards perceived obligations too compelling to resist? Was it hard to resist doing what you felt you should do?

- The next time you get the chance for a "flow day" you could add another layer of intention. This time, as you start your day, make conscious decisions

about how you would like to spend it. What is important to you? You have a day. Think of it as a work of art to create. Whereas during the first day you had no pre-planned ideas or expectations about the day, you just flowed from one thing to the next according to your whim, this time start out with intentions of how you intend to fill your hours. What form does your unique creativity take? Then allow the day to flow in the same way as before. Let each part of the day unfold in its own time, take as much time as it needs. At the end of the day, take stock. Of all your initial intentions, which ones were realized?
- Record what you observe after a few flow days when habitual routines were paused. Try to incorporate some moments of spontaneity in each day. Habitual behaviors can be wonderfully efficient. They can also be numbing.
- Remember that each day is a microcosm of your whole life.

Leave your comfort zone

Try something new.

I am eternally grateful to one of my High School teachers who required that each week students "have a new experience" and write about it. The only requirement was that it had to be something we had never, ever done before. And we had to do it alone!

I tried an archeological dig, a seance, an anthropological meeting, a group therapy session and more. We learnt new ideas and skills, we met new people but more importantly, we learnt about ourselves.

Try things that naturally attract you and things that don't. Put yourself in situations that are as varied as possible and watch. Use your local paper for ideas. The very newness of these experiences will illuminate what attracts you and what bores you.

Write your legacy

Fast forward. You died. What have you left behind? How will you be remembered? Will you be remembered? Who will remember you? What are you creating now in your life that will remain? Property, money, investments, art, businesses, beauty, objects, systems, inventions, children, goodwill, change, friendship, love?

- How would you like to be remembered? What would you like people to say about you after you're gone?
- Write the legacy you would like to leave. What is important to you to be remembered for?
- Even if you are young, would you feel a sense of completion if you were to die tomorrow?
- What things are you putting off?
- On your deathbed, what will bring a smile to your lips and allow you to murmur: "Well, that was a life well lived." If you were to die tomorrow, would you say that? Are there still things to be done? Why are you waiting?

For many years I had a sticker on my fridge reading: How soon is NOW? It made me realize how I procrastinated, made excuses to do things next week, next year... next life?

The sticker changed my procrastination and when I caught myself looking forward to things, I tried hard to start the process of making them happen. It worked. I recommend that sticker. It encourages you to prioritize and to realize your priorities.

- Take time to reflect. Then write your legacy.
- Use this as inspiration to design your next chapter.

Books, Magazines, TED talks, movies etc.

Keep a record of when you make a value decision. Whether choosing magazines, books, films, or Ted talks, deciding where to eat or have coffee or shop, notice what attracts you, how you decide.

Do you love the new or the familiar?

If you gravitate to what you know, try something new. If you always go for the new, try returning to the familiar and see how that feels.

Try choosing things that don't attract you and see if sometimes you are pleasantly surprised.

Challenge your mind with new information, lay down new neural pathways and watch the unknown become your new known.

Above all, notice when you feel most completely yourself, at home. Notice when whatever the stimuli, it gives you a sense of you, and who you want to become. Reaffirm who you are and discover that you could be more. Rediscover what you love.

Unique Ability

Ask yourself the question:

"What Am I good at?"

Maybe you're good at a lot of things. List them.

Then ask yourself the question:

"What do I like being good at? Which of the things I am good at, matter most to me?" List those.

There is an excellent book entitled "Unique Ability" by Catherine Nomura and Julia Waller. They start with the suggestion that you simply ask the people who know you best what your unique abilities are. In trepidation I sent the letter they offer in their text to 8 people who know me well. The consistency of the replies was startling and made me realize that however doubting we may be ourselves, others seem to see us well.

They then suggest you ask yourself:

"What are my best habits? How do I consistently get my best results?

Once you have some ideas about:
- what you are good at
- what you like being good at
- your most effective habits

- You can try formulating a statement that describes your unique ability.

"The essence of what you do well and the underlying passion that motivates and drives you."

Unique Ability.   Catherine Nomura and Julia Waller

Do this repeatedly because most of us are complex and have several abilities that are unique to us.

The question then becomes: What percentage of my time do I spend using my unique abilities? How could I use them more often?

Allow new people to inspire your desire

Bring new people into your sphere.

When did you last make a new friend?

How many strangers do you talk to each day?

What would it take to turn an acquaintance into a friend?

How many friends do you have from totally other walks of life than your own?

How many friends do you have with totally other opinions or interests than your own?

How many friends do you have who are older or younger than you? Do you have friends in each decade?

As we go through life, it is too easy for our sphere of personal interaction to become increasingly homogeneous. We have children and our friends become other parents. We get a job and our friends become our colleagues.

When we are with our intimates and familiars, so much of what they know about us has been laid down over the years and is now assumed.

When we meet new people, they start with a blank slate. Nothing about us is known or assumed. Possibly we have evolved over the years into someone who is in fact somewhat different from the person our intimates know. With someone new, we can start from scratch again, and be seen afresh. This is not to say that our intimates are wrong about us, but it is possibly different for them to assimilate changes in us as they arise.

Interacting with people you have just met allows you to glimpse into a unique mirror of yourself. And it offers a glimpse into other lives, other perspectives, opinions, other ways of being in the world. All of this may awaken sides of yourself you were previously unaware of.

- Make a point of talking to as many diverse people as you can. Some can be those who you feel really attracted to, others maybe the opposite. Note what you learn about them and about yourself. What surprises do you get? Can you tell how people see you? Is that how you want to be seen?
- Take the risk of intimacy. Whereas small talk is often inevitable, it can often be a wasted

opportunity. If appropriate, take conversation to a deeper level. This may result in wonderful insights into how someone else's mind and heart works and may lead you to deepen your own sense of who you are in relation to them. If you ask questions about what is important to them, you may both benefit from the discussion and gain new insight. For instance, you may simply ask: "What's uppermost for you at the moment?" "What are you looking forward to?" "What is most fulfilling for you at the moment?"

- This won't be possible for all but if you get the chance, go on a trip alone with people you don't know. Spending longer periods of time with strangers is an even better way to learn about yourself, and others.

The Unlived Life

"Unlived life does not just go away through underuse or by tossing it off and thinking that what we have abandoned is no longer useful or relevant. Of course, no-one can live out all of life's possibilities, but there are KEY aspects of your being that must be brought into your life, or you will never realize your fulfillment"

Living Your Unlived Life.

Robert A. Johnson and Jerry Ruhl Ph.D.

This is the time to pay attention to the key aspects of your being that are, as yet, unlived. There may be things you haven't yet done or been that you haven't even thought of. There may be things you really wanted long ago but over the years have forgotten.

- Notice when you say: "I really regret that I didn't...." or "I regret that I haven't been...." Make notes of what it is you regret not having done, or how you haven't been. Can you do it, be it, now? If you were to die tomorrow, would there be things you regret not having done? If so, do or become it. Consider both missed opportunities, things you didn't do and personal traits you haven't developed, creativity, empathy, patience, humor, contentment, etc. Of course, we can't "do" everything, nor can we "be" everything. But look for key aspects of your life that are, as yet, unlived.

Sit in stillness with your breath and ask yourself:

- What would I do or be if I knew I couldn't fail? Fear of failure is often the reason we don't explore an avenue that excites and draws us. If we succumb to this fear the desire, the attraction, will fade.

    When you ask this question, you may experience qualities of who you are that have been dormant. They may arise just as feelings with no words. Acknowledge these feelings as they surface and allow yourself to expand into them. From this, new directions will appear.

Peak Experiences

Reflect on the Peak Experiences of your life: the moments you will remember until the day you die.... the moments that have made it all worthwhile. The ones that stand apart from all the other days, months, even years that merge into indistinguishable, forgettable acres of time.

What is it you remember?

Why?

How did you feel at that time?

What was it in you that came alive?

What part of you was touched?

Make a list of those experiences. It may be that you do not, at this stage of your life, need to replicate those experiences but analyze what it was about them that makes them stand out.

What would it take to have more of that in your life?

Notice how money affects your desire.

Money is so intricately entangled with who we've become over the years, that to even ask the question: "What would you do if money were no object," most probably seems ridiculous at first glance. Most of us have become so conditioned to take financial considerations into account as a first response that we don't even look seriously at the question. Of course, money is an issue, but it is interesting, for this purpose of discovering what you really want, to pretend it isn't! It's interesting to fantasize, momentarily, how life might be if money really were not an issue.

If we always approach possibilities from the point of view of "Can I afford it?" or rather, "I can't afford it", doors will close even before they fully open. A nascent germ of inspiration will be nipped in the bud. We will limit our options before we even start to get creative about ways to finance them. If we take money into account each time an idea arrives, 90% of our ideas will never even reach the table. That is limiting!

Start from the other end.

"What would you do if there were no financial limitations?"

Ask this not to encourage excess, profligate extravagance, decadence, and gluttony, but simply to shift your perspective.

You can spend ample time later being realistic and creative with the finance.

Have fun and make a list.

And now....

What have you learned from this? Where have all these questions led you? Have you felt any sense of coming home to who you are, what you want? Did you unearth buried places where your Life-Force shone out, through the questions? Have you tasted the uniqueness of your soul?

Above all, can you simultaneously dive into the pool of well-being deep inside you and be ready to expand into your life's next chapter?

Where are you now? Do you have even a vague sense of what draws you, inspires you? Are you still in the dark or are you quite clear and ready to start?

If you are still looking at that blank canvas, just take more time. Often new ways of seeing yourself in the world take a long time to materialize.

If you are bubbling over with ideas, embrace them and notice, over time, which ones have traction and which fade, if any.

If you are overwhelmed, take a break but keep your Witness alive and notice what pops back into your heart when you're not even looking.

If fear arises, remember that you can take "small steps", once something feels right, and proceed with ease.

What has been your experience so far? Did you have distinct moments of "knowing", "gut reactions", "aha" moments, or are things evolving slowly, with gentle glimmerings of insight?

Are you starting to touch your heart's desire?

What do you feel may be on its way, a complete overhaul, or a modest tweak? Are you craving a big shift or a modest addition? Do you yearn for a big splash of crimson or a subtle shade of grey on the tapestry of your life? What will make it yours? Maybe all you need is more stillness to feel the joy that is deep within you.

Give yourself plenty of time to allow your feelings to settle, your insights to clarify. The next step is to write.

- Write down, right now, what you feel to be true. It can be general or specific, clear, or vague. What ignites your Life-Force?

Undoubtedly what you write now will change before you take a single step, so allow creative juices to flow, you will not be held to a single word!

Over the next few days and weeks, revisit what you write, frequently. If your truth has shifted, write what's new and keep it all. Somewhere along the way, some or all of it may turn out to be the gem you need.

The written word solidifies your thoughts and reveals what is real and what is not.

The spoken word takes this to yet another level.

- When you are ready, share your thoughts with someone else. When you articulate your thoughts with conviction you will hear it in your voice. When you hear your truth, it is powerful and exhilarating. You will also hear if it is not true as your voice will be weak, unconvincing. If this is the case, admit it.

Gradually you will arrive at a statement that is true and exciting. You anticipate stepping back onto the path that is uniquely, specifically yours.

Take time here to celebrate!

There will be issues to resolve, there may be anxieties, doubts and uncertainties, failures, false starts to face, problems to solve, but celebrate that you have once again, touched your soul.

Above all there may be negativity from others. For whatever reason it can be threatening to other people when someone they know decides to make changes. They'll remind you of the dangers, the risks, the uncertainty, and the possible failures. If you too are still feeling uncertain and scared, this can be enough to stop you in your tracks. Listen to what they have to say, thank them for their concern, understand that they probably wish they were able to make changes too. Then stick to your process.

Once you have accepted your new reality and feel increasingly comfortable with it, you may feel the urge to forge ahead, take control and start making things happen. I urge you not to. Control after all is a fallacy and try as we may, life seems to have a habit of just happening.

So, don't rush to implement decisions, choices. Just hold them as a new possible reality and watch what unfolds. Having planted the seed, it will germinate.

Get out of your own way and allow life to happen. It will. Don't force it, there's no need. But do respond if you feel energy to make a move, to take action...just be sure the impetus is yours. Take off the clamps and allow expansion to happen. Allow spontaneity.

Control is never achieved when vigorously sought after. It is the surprising outcome of letting go.

For a while relish these new feelings of desire, of wanting. When the moment is right a step will be taken, a step that is uniquely yours.

Chapter 4 - *Your Money Psychology*

"Money provides a direct inroad into our psyche. It can be an invaluable teacher if we watch how it manipulates, controls, inspires and excites us. Watch yourself as you deal with it on a daily basis".

Money and the Meaning of Life. Jacob Needleman.

In the previous chapter all financial concerns were on hold as we explored desire. Our focus was entirely on awakening your Life -Force.

Now we gladly reintroduce the other partner in this relationship, money, and marry the two: we connect money and soul. The remainder of this book will approach the two as intimately entwined.

I'll start with a look at who you are as a money being, your Money psychology. Just as each of us is driven by a completely unique Life Force, so each of us has a unique relationship to money. It is impossible, in our culture, *not* to have a relationship with money. Some proclaim that money is unimportant, for others it drives their every waking moment. Wherever you are on this spectrum, no-one completely escapes the power of money at some point.

As someone who has found herself at times working exclusively for money, not passion, I certainly envy those who are able to provide for themselves financially by following their passion.

For the rest of us, the journey is often more nuanced.

Life can bombard us with endless decisions that pit money against our passion, financial security against our dreams. Sometimes it is possible to find a middle way, keep both threads alive, and compromise. But often, as the years slip by, many people start to feel a nagging disconnect between what they once dreamed of, and the way life is.

Do you?

Our relationship to money can slowly but surely lead us away from our essential core. We may even start to conflate money with feelings of self-worth! The accumulation of money can become all consuming, and our notions of the life we once longed to live, atrophy and fade. One of my teachers once said to me:

"Our money issues are linked so closely to our ego that if we clear them all we would be very close to waking up".

Here you will observe your thoughts, beliefs, feelings, and behaviors about money that have been formed throughout your childhood and by life experience. We each have our own money "script" and it is our intention in this chapter to shine a light on yours.

You will use the same skills of Noticing and Presence as you watch yourself with curiosity engage in financial transactions. You will learn to recognize habitual behaviors and emotions. As you spend, give, receive, borrow, or invest you will watch closely your responses and behavior until you become intimately familiar with yourself as a money person. You will begin to see what makes you tick around money, maybe even smiling to yourself as you once again, for example, go for the cheapest (or most expensive) item on the menu...

This exploration will give you precious insights that may bring you more peace of mind and joy in your current reality, even if no change is happening for you at this time.

As a Planner, it was my job to get to know how each of my clients functioned psychologically with money and to help them understand this relationship themselves. Only then could they make decisions that were truly authentic for them, decisions that freed their souls, and provided the security they needed.

They soon discovered, (as will you), that wherever life took them, the journey was smoother, less stressful, when they understood their money psychology.

Now is the time to take a long and deep look at your relationship with money and the part it has played in the evolution of who you have become. Or possibly, who you have *not* become.

And as you contemplate life changes, the importance of your relationship with money will be heightened. Money can easily sabotage your plans for change. From joining a gym to starting a corporation, you will need to reassess your financial situation. This may be unsettling, and excuses may creep in and wreak havoc with your plans.

So the goal, as with all relationships, is to create respect, balance, and equanimity with money. If money holds too much power over you, you may end up its slave. If, on the other hand, you have no respect for money and pay it little attention, you may find yourself penniless and anxious. If you fear its power, you may simply reject it and deny its importance

Ask yourself, regarding money: "Who has control?" If *you* do, money is an essential tool that opens you to opportunity and experience. If *it* does, it keeps you scared, instinctively turning from possibility, potentially trapped in the wrong life.

To compound all this, our relationship with money is, of course, totally one sided. Money certainly does not have a relationship with you! Money is, after all, simply a medium of exchange whose value fluctuates as a result of supply and demand. It is inanimate and only has the value that we attribute to it. Strange then, the power it can wield.

As life presents a series of daily decisions, your relationship with money is constantly in play. Each decision you face, be it small: Americano or Cappuccino, or large: accepting the job offer or not, will involve money, and reveal insight into your values and desires. The insidious way money orchestrates each detail of your life can reveal deep emotional vulnerabilities.

Becoming familiar with those vulnerabilities, *and their origin*, the power they have over you, will enable you to do the principal work of this book: be open to creative solutions to design the life you want *with the financial security you need*. Not one or the other, both.

The consequences of not doing this work are considerable if your nascent plans, however large or small, are to take shape.

If you allow fear and need for safety to dictate your decisions, you will stay safe, possibly at the expense of the life you would love to inhabit.

If you blatantly ignore fear in fits of financial bravado, you may end up bankrupt and miserable.

Jacob Needleman, in his book: "Money and the Meaning of Life" describes a workshop he had given on this topic. Towards the end of the workshop, he had invited the students to send him a question, in writing, about money, any question that had come to them over the course of the workshop about their relationship with money. He had asked primarily for economic, academic questions.

Here are some of the of the responses:

"How much of myself will I have to sell for money in order to be able to live more fully later, and can I regain what I've sold?"

"There is something very frightening about money. I don't understand it. So, apparently, it is not only a material entity, but is tied to inner psychological forces. What can I do to see clearly what money really means?"

"How can I let go of my fears about money- it totally absorbs my consciousness. I fear I will get old and become a street person?"

"What is money a substitute for in my essential nature? Why do I attach myself to it as something necessary to my life? What do I confuse it with ?"

"Why does spending money cause me so much pain?"

"Why am I so angry that the distribution of wealth is so polarized? Why does it make me feel so exposed, so helpless?"

These searching questions reveal the depths of emotional anguish money can trigger.

- What would your Money question be if invited to ask one?
- Which of the questions above resonates most with you?

"Money is like an iron ring we put through our nose. It is now leading us around wherever it wants. We just forgot that we are the ones who designed it".

The Good Men Project. Mark Kinney

What is *your* relationship with money and why did you design it that way?

The following exercises will guide you towards a healthy, cooperative relationship so that, whatever your financial situation, it will be your ally as you create the life you want.

You can choose to write or speak your responses, but if you write, I encourage you to share your insights with a partner or friend. Dig deep into your memory and record anything that strikes a significant chord.

We will start, once again, by retracing the past.

Exercises

Your Money Autobiography

This exercise will give insight into how, over the years, you have become the Money Person you are.

Write a history of your relationship with money from your earliest memory to present time. You may want to write freely, or you may want to refer to some of the following ideas. These suggestions may help you scratch the surface of how your money identity has been built, but don't limit yourself, allow your mind to wander in its own direction. If you want, don't even use these questions, just write your story.

- *Your family's financial situation throughout your life.*

- *Your parents' attitude to money as you remember it throughout your life.*
- *How you felt about your family's financial status compared to others.*
- *Have you ever been ashamed or proud of yourself around money?*
- *Your financial situation since you have been independent.*
- *How do you relate to people who have more or less money than you?*
- *How you feel about receiving gifts of money or giving gifts of money.*
- *What has been your money theme? What is your script?*
- *What has been your form of money madness? Do you have one?*
- *What have been your spending patterns?*
- *Are you generous or miserly?*
- *Who have you blamed for your money issues?*
- *What is usually the cause of disagreements about money?*
- *Have you generally felt poor or prosperous?*
- *What have your major financial blunders been?*

Now scan back over your autobiography and pull out a few of the major themes or patterns that most significantly resonate with you. Notice the ones that grab your attention or that cause an emotional reaction.

Write them down.

Under each pattern, write an action that would reverse this behavior for you, and do it. See how you feel when you do it. See how you feel when you even think about doing it.

For example: if your pattern is normally to be miserly, reverse it by paying the toll at a toll booth for the next three drivers and see how it feels.

Or, if your pattern is to use money to buy approval from family and friends, give an anonymous gift instead and see how that feels.

If your pattern is to blame another person for your money issues, try taking responsibility for the issue yourself. Try to forgive the other person, learn what you can from the experience and move on.

- If you could do any part of your autobiography over again, what would you change?
- What would your ideal money autobiography look like?
- Can you now trace your relationship to money back through your life experience?
- Can you follow the thread of your current beliefs and vulnerabilities back to their genesis?
- Can you see how you have evolved into the money being that you now are?

Can you step back from that and see that YOU are not that person, it is only a set of behaviors and attitudes that have been imprinted on you throughout your life experience?

In order to go still deeper into discovering who you have become (or not become) in relation to Money, we return to your Life Map.

The Life Map

Here we will expand on the list of "Turning Points" you made in Chapter 2.

- Look back at the Life Map you made in Chapter 2. Expand it, add to it, and give explanations and background to each turning point. Focus particularly on the relevance of money at each turning point.

As you face the decisions you made, notice the ones that you now regret and those that enlivened you. It may be painful to look at "missteps" but try to welcome them as periods where you learnt in the most powerful way, how you became for a while, who you are not, and followed paths that led in the wrong direction.

Notice the role that **money** played in each of these decisions, these transitions in your life that sent you in a different direction. It is important to track them and shine light on the impetus behind them. As you look back at them you will probably know immediately if they were right or wrong, if they moved you further along "your" path or whether they were made as a result of fear, lack, or insecurity. Take note of the impetus behind the decisions you later regretted.

If you stepped off your path, have you been able to make a U-turn or have you headed further and further down the wrong track until you possibly lost sight of the right one and ultimately who you are?

I'll give a couple of examples from my own life at which I made life changing decisions. Some sent me in the right direction, some in the wrong. The challenge has been to notice the wrong turns, recognize them, and endeavor to make corrections.

Age 21:

Newly graduated, I took a position as teacher although I had never intended to teach. I had intended to use my degree in Education and English Literature to become a journalist. But I was too scared of not being able to make money from my own devices. I was too scared of not being able to get a job as a journalist. Too scared of the unknown. Too scared of appearing as if I couldn't support myself.

Also at this age:

Married a man as a result of fear of doing life, money etc. on my own. I knew it wouldn't last. I went through with it because I needed the "security" of making decisions together. Also, because my parents had already spent thousands on the wedding!

Age 28:

Jumped at the opportunity to share in construction and sailing of a catamaran and embarked on a 3-year adventure. Very risky financial proposition but felt 100% alive, excited, free, and creative.

Age 40:

While teaching ESL at Canadian University I was offered full tenure and benefits. I was faced head on with the conflict between "security" and who I was. I turned down the position and was filled with a sense of freedom and possibility.

Age 45:

Felt growing anxiety about lack of regular income. I started blaming others for this. I then joined a group of women to start a business. I felt a sense of financial independence and control that I craved. And I found sides to myself that I never suspected I had.

I have been able to identify about 8 turning points so far. Each one was highly informative about the power money has held over me and how strongly it influenced many decisions I made.

With more awareness of how money was influencing my decisions, maybe I would have been able to defer big decisions until I had more experience, until I had got my feet wet in the enormous puddle of life.

I hope that your Life Map and Autobiography provide insight for you into how and why things have happened as they did. They don't have to continue in the same way.

Risk/Anxiety

Some of the most powerful components of any relationship with money are risk and anxiety.

What is risk and why are some of us attracted to it and some repelled by it?

Risk is a double-edged sword. If we consider risk to represent the possibility of loss, we will turn away from it and try to stay safe. If, however, we consider taking a risk to be opening a door to possibility, then we may embrace it. How do *you* respond to risk? How well do you understand your emotional reaction to it?

"Excuses are lullabies that hold us back from living fully. When we don't take risks, we stay stuck in a box of routine and familiarity. Dull, uninspired. It takes courage to take a risk because we have to confront our deepest fears and limited beliefs about what is possible. But the rewards are great. Taking risks expands our comfort zone by creating different neural pathways and experiences for us that become our new known. It makes life juicy, we feel more alive".

"Your Presence is Enough." Julia Tindall.

So, these questions arise:

- Do you welcome risk as an opportunity even if it challenges your security?
- Do you reject risky propositions even if it means staying stuck in routine and familiarity?
- In general, where do you land on that spectrum?

Each of us will have a different answer in each different situation. The work here is to know yourself well enough so that your response to risk is authentic. Learning to recognize when your decision is authentic requires introspection and self-inquiry.

There is no objective right or wrong in any situation. Arguably the only "wrong" is if your reactions, when opportunity arises, are not honest: those situations when your heart is screaming "Yes", but because of habit, fear, conditioning, you respond with a "No". Or when your heart is screaming "No", but because of peer pressure, expectations, or habit, you respond with a "Yes".

If you are someone who feels deadened by the "box of routine and familiarity", then accepting change if it beckons, may be your challenge. If you feel anxious at the notion of change, then your challenge is to create steps that are realistic for you in a timeframe you can handle. Change inevitably requires facing the unknown. Self-knowledge is the only way to manage the unknown, smoothly.

As you move through each transition in life, each change, some of the unknown you encounter will inevitably be financial. So, whether your planning requires simply opening a savings account or whether it requires dealing with sophisticated financial systems, it is essential not only to have an awareness of the inherent risk of each, but also an awareness of your own reactions when dealing with those risks.

Understanding financial risk is complex. In a later chapter we will look in depth at the risks of each financial strategy. Here we look at your emotional reaction to it. Only with both pieces will you pick your solutions that are right for you and allow risk to become your opportunity. The rewards of taking risk may be exponential, but if you can't handle the psychological repercussions, taking too much risk (for you) may be devastating.

If you take too little risk (for you) and life becomes dull, you may feel a creeping anxiety that life is slipping by, that you are not living fully.

If you take too much risk (for you), you suffer fear of loss.

I cannot overestimate the power of financial anxiety, and the resulting risk avoidance if too much risk is taken. Fear of losing money from a practical point of view is one thing, but the psychological repercussions of financial loss can be far-reaching. They may include loss of self-esteem, loss of self-respect, loss of friendships, family, material comfort, success and ultimately loss of life.

Therefore, choosing appropriate financial strategies is essential, and requires carefully matching risk tolerance with psychological makeup.

Some of us are lucky enough to live quite peacefully with money, with our financial situation.

Others of us live our whole lives bowing at the feet of the money god, terrified of its power! Who has the upper hand in your relationship with money? Does the money god have her boney fingers clasped around your neck so that each decision is made to release the grip, subjugating your judgement and desire to its pressure?

I hope to put you in control, so that money becomes a facilitator of whatever steps you take through life. Use the following inquiries to better understand your own relationship to risk and the situations that trigger anxiety.

Record your responses to the following questions. Make sure that each time you experience anxiety about money, you record it in a notebook. Be as specific as possible about both the particulars of the situation and the anxiety it arouses.

- Think of times in the past when you have felt anxious about money. What was the situation that caused the anxiety? Were you taking a large loan? Were you short of income? Did you make a risky investment? There are many more possibilities.
- Now ask yourself about the deeper cause of the problem. Does your anxiety stem from the fact that you have overextended your current obligations without understanding your own capacity for risk? Or does it more often stem from the fact that you are craving more from life and the very thought of change can arouse intense anxiety about the financial implications of making change. Which is most often the cause of your anxiety (maybe your money autobiography can be useful here).
- On a deeper level still, can you trace the source or origin of the anxiety? Does it stem from childhood experience, the way you were raised? Or does it stem from experiences that have impacted you as an adult?

What form does your anxiety take? Do you bottle it up? Do you brush it under the carpet? Do you bore everyone with it? Do you comfort yourself with food or drink? Do you lose sleep? If the anxiety causes sleeplessness, it is almost certainly time to start paying close attention. Maybe a solution is in this book, maybe you need to seek other help or just talk to friends and family about it. But there is a solution and once you recognize the problem you are on the way to solving it.

One of the most anxious times in my life was when I took the risk of giving up my teaching career.

This is what happened...

I had spent 4 years at University, I had spent years trying different jobs, I had started to climb the ladder of promotion, I was making decent money. But for years I knew. This was not the career for me. After an extended period of simply having no "joie de vivre", of waiting for each weekend, I finally acknowledged my Truth. I finally allowed myself to articulate what I had known for ages. I did not want to be a schoolteacher. This was so hard to say, so hard to think. But when I did, I felt a remarkable lightness. My whole being relaxed, I was smiling at life again, smiling at all the adventures in store for me. But I was terrified. All I knew was what I didn't want, but initially I had no clue what I did want. There were no answers, just the unknown, not an easy place to be. So, whenever anxiety arose, I tried to remember that the process of transition could take as long as it needed, that to some extent I could manage the risk, if I stayed true to the decision. Soon opportunities started to open for me.

Getting real about money worries, even if we do nothing about them for a while, is very freeing.

Security

The inverse of risk and a second essential component of our relationship to money, is our need for security.

What is security?

Security implies freedom from danger or threat, which we would assume is always a good thing. But our need for security, and how it is satisfied, is subjective and very personal. And it is essential to understand our individual need for security before making significant life changes.

Some of us feel insecure when faced with the unknown because we imagine that things will not turn out well.

Others seem able to approach change with optimism, assuming that everything will be fine!

It is natural, when anticipating a life-change, to feel some insecurity, either because of leaping into the unknown or by having to face some financial upheaval.

Whenever outcomes are uncertain, and insecurity is experienced, plans risk being abandoned. It is therefore essential to become familiar with your own need for security and the emotional turmoil that can result if you cross your safety threshold.

By using your Witness, start to pay special attention to your feelings when faced with situations that are new and the outcome is unknown. Feeling insecure for an extended period may easily be detrimental to your health. But if the situation passes quickly, like giving a speech or doing an interview, it may be bearable. Long term financial insecurity, however, can eat away at your self-esteem and confidence leaving you exhausted and unable to break free. So, it is vital to recognize and acknowledge these feelings before making major decisions.

Reflect deeply as you consider the following inquiries:
- What does security mean to you?
- What have you learnt throughout your life about your relationship with security?
- When have you felt insecure?
- How did feelings of insecurity affect your behavior?
- Remember a time when you either accepted or refused to take a financial risk. How did that feel at the time? How did your behavior reflect your feelings?

For most of us, honoring both our need for security *and* keeping life juicy is challenging.

We need to discover if we are compromising our need for security too much in order to live fully or if we are compromising Life Force too much for security. Security and juiciness need to be happily entwined, balanced.

The security/insecurity spectrum covers a wide range of issues. Consider these questions about security.

- Can you feel secure if you are hungry and cold?
- Can you feel secure if you are living the wrong life?
- Can you feel secure without owning a home, car, and portfolio?
- Can you feel secure if your primary relationship is dull?

How would you rank those potential insecurities for you? What else holds the potential of instilling feelings of insecurity in you?

We see that security is a multifaceted creature wrapped up in issues of status, power, love and, of course, money and it is important to understand your unique needs for each of them.

The renowned psychologist Abraham Maslow addressed the concept of security when he identified a hierarchy of "needs" as a pyramid, with physical needs (food, clothing, shelter) on the base, followed by emotional needs (love, belonging, esteem) and self-actualization at the top. His theory states that only when the basic physical and emotional needs are satisfied, can we reach for the gem, self-actualization.

The inquiry for us here is to reflect upon the value we put on self-actualization as compared to the infinite ways of satisfying the physical and emotional needs. For instance, we can choose to satisfy our need for food with beans and rice or we can choose steak and caviar. The lucky ones of us have a choice. We can strive for a castle or settle for a bungalow. We can earn the admiration of others with designer clothes, houses, boats and planes or a friendly phone call and a cup of coffee.

The choices are endless. Where do your priorities fall in terms of physical and emotional security?

Do you prefer to settle for modest material wealth in favor of self-actualization? Does the accumulation of material assets absorb you to the exclusion of self-actualization? Or is the beauty of material assets your path to self-actualization?

Where do you draw the line? What *does* make your heart sing?

Finding your own path to security and self-actualization is individual and completely entangled with your money psychology. It is also often instilled in us over our lifetime and is the result of what we experience along the way.

What would it take to allow you to feel secure enough so you could also reach for self-actualization, *and* have the freedom to explore new realms of possibility?

Beliefs

"Your beliefs become your thoughts,

Your thoughts become your words,

Your words become your actions,

Your actions become your habits,

Your habits become your values,

Your values become your destiny."

— Mahatma Gandhi

We could add a further line to Gandhi's wisdom above: "Your destiny becomes who you are."

The question then becomes: Is the way you live your life an authentic expression of your true beliefs and values? Are they truly *your* beliefs and values?

Our money beliefs are molded and sculpted subtly over our entire life so that by the time we become adults they are usually so built in, so habitual, it is hard to recognize our "self" as separate from them.

In this section we have started to unearth your deep-rooted, ingrained beliefs about money and questioned the validity of each one to see which are still true, still serve you and which limit, constrict, or wrongly define your life.

When you "witness" a thought as you prepare to articulate a belief, you have a chance to question its truth. If your thoughts, (and words) are true, then your actions also stand a better chance of being authentic. But if you too frequently trot out "truisms" about money that are no longer your true beliefs, then you literally risk living the wrong life.

Here is a personal example of a belief I once held, but managed to see its falsehood for me:

I used to hold the belief that people who were wealthier than me would automatically be critical of me, and therefore reject me. Consequently, I never pursued friendships with people that I perceived to be better off than I. I seriously limited the choice of people I allowed into my life. I played it safe. I believed that having less was synonymous with *being* less. This belief sadly limited the range of people I allowed into my heart.

Gradually, the more I was able to examine and understand the origins of these beliefs, the easier it was to navigate through them. Once I saw how this fallacy had been baked into my development, it fell away and now some of my closest friends are people I had instinctively avoided.

I have quite often observed people who truly believe they can earn respect and approval from others by appearing well-off.

Our beliefs and values about money are built into us in one way or another from the day we are born. And as we grow, we receive strong messages from parents, relatives, friends, and our culture. Our language is filled with money "truisms" that probably impact our consciousness more than we'd care to admit. Here are just a few:

Waste not want not.

Can't buy me love.

Neither a lender nor a borrower be.

You get what you pay for.

A fool and his money are easily parted.

Better to be miserable rich than miserable poor.

Money is the root of all evil.

Can't spoil a good thing.

You can't miss what you never had.

Notice which ones of these you have somehow taken on board, subliminally, as your own.

Can you think of others?

- Write down the money beliefs you were raised with, the money messages you received consistently from your parents either in words or by modeling.

Let's look now at more personal beliefs about money that may have become ingrained in you over the years:

Do you consider yourself rich or poor?

Do you believe that will ever change?

Do you want it to change?

Do you believe people respect you more if you appear wealthy?

Do you believe you should behave as your parents did with money?

Do you believe people judge you as "privileged" if you have more money than them?

Do you believe it is your role to support your family?

Do you believe you deserve the best?

Do you believe you will only get the best if some element of suffering is involved i.e., a job you dislike?

Do you believe you can never have too much money?

Do you believe in delayed gratification?

Do you believe that if you have money, you should spend it or save it?

Do you believe poor people are lazy?

Do you believe rich people are spoiled/entitled? Where is your bias with those last 2 questions?

Which of those "beliefs" have the most charge for you? What other beliefs about money spring to your mind that you believe to be true?

You will learn a lot about your money beliefs if you start to *notice* what you say each time you make a statement or ask a question that in any way relates to money. The more emphatically you make an assertion, the more important it is to question it.

If we accept that what we believe becomes what we say, and what we say becomes what we do, then it is only a small step to seeing that eventually our habits become what we value, and our destiny is a direct result of our thinking.

Notice what you think! ...

What are your beliefs about financial status?

- Does perceived financial status affect how you interact with or judge others? Do you feel more (or less) confident with people you think are richer (or poorer) than you?

- Is your sense of self-worth or self-esteem stronger when you think you are doing well financially?
- Do you feel embarrassed around people less "successful" than you? Do you underplay your success?
- Do you feel shame when you are around people more successful than you?
- Do you try to compete?

Values

Do your habits reflect your values?

What were your values before those habits were formed? Once things become habitual, they become hard to change, we question them less and therefore they unconsciously distort our destiny.

It's too easy to become who we are not.

It's relatively easy to know your habits if you watch yourself move through your days. But values? They can sometimes get lost in the demands of all these habitual actions! It is harder to stay in touch with your values and therefore to see if your daily behavior reflects what you really value. Habits become your values. But what were your values before you developed those habits?

- Reflect over your life and jot down any values you may have had in the past. Do you still value those things? Have some fallen away? Why?
- Make a list of your current values, noticing those that are new and those that persist maybe from childhood/youth.

Allow yourself as much time as you need for this. Possibly many will come flooding out initially, but if you allow a week or so for completion you may end up with a more full and richer picture of your value system. Reminisce. Remember childhood, adolescence. What did you value then? Does remembering them rekindle a passion? Allow it to be broad. What really matters to you?

Having completed the list, ask:

- Are you living your values?

Unlived values are not values.

Or maybe they are just dormant. What would it take to rekindle them, incorporate more of them into your life now?

Notice if there is a connection between money and a dormant value.

Notice how often you blame money for not doing something you value. Notice when you say:

I can't afford it.

It's a waste of money.

I'm saving for something.

It takes too much capital to do that.

I wouldn't waste money on extravagances like that.

I'll think about that when x, y or z happens.

How many things are there on the list that you really value that are not in your life right now? Why not?

If one of your values is a healthy environment, when did you last volunteer to help restore local walking trails? Or write to your council about the spraying of the curbside weeds?

If one of your values is art, when did you last visit a gallery? Paint a picture?

If one of your values is travel, when did you last take a trip? Even a bus ride to the next town.

Getting involved with things that mean a lot to you means meeting like-minded people who can inspire and guide you back to a life you value.

- One quick way to check up on yourself is to scan through your checkbook or credit card records and find out exactly how you spend money. Obviously, if you value long hikes in Nature, those, thankfully like writing to your representative or volunteering, are free.

If you love food, do you buy and eat the food that interests, delights, and nourishes you?

If you love music, what part does it play in your life?

If you love to dance, climb, scuba dive, sing, do you do it?

If you value friendship, how are you building those relationships?

Ask yourself to what extent a decision not to pursue what you value is causing a separation from who you once were. Ask if there is a way to reignite those values without causing yourself stress about money. There usually is.

To nourish your values is to nourish yourself.

Aligning directly to your values will smooth the path that leads to the destiny that is yours.

Living your destiny will determine who you are. Are you becoming who you are? Or who you are not?

Your Money Script

Our beliefs and values, together with our fears, needs, anxieties and habits gradually meld into our "money script", the script that defines who we are as a money person.

In this section, you will reveal your money script, question it, maybe step away from it and towards a more open, free, and evolving relationship with money.

Our script starts being written right from early childhood when we are told: "Put that down, we can't afford it", or "We'll have the expensive one, you always get what you pay for". It evolves as we grow and are told that the equipment for this or that sport is too expensive or asked exactly which country we would like to travel to on our foreign exchange. It is again reinforced as we make college choices, or have them made for us. And so it goes.

Eventually, these accumulated messages have an effect on us; an inclination towards being thrifty or a spendthrift, a workaholic or a "get rich quicker", a giver or an accumulator, generous or stingy, etc. Your script will emerge, and you will learn to recognize it.

Our money script may change as we move through life and our circumstances change, but any script, like any habit, benefits from illumination.

- Pay close attention each time you notice yourself thinking or speaking about anything that involves money and observe your pattern over time. Your money script will be revealed.

Once you understand your money script you can smile at it, and decide each time a money issue arises, whether to read your script or respond more authentically in that moment.

This takes practice as there are usually powerful reasons that our script is as it is. Sometimes we simply adopt the money script of our parents but often our script is a defensive reaction to a circumstance that was in some way painful like the following:

- The child who was always made to feel not good enough by his parents and then moves into adulthood with the need to accumulate vast sums of money to prove his worth.

- The child whose home was one of scarcity and as an adult can never feel there is enough, so is overly frugal.
- The child whose life was stiflingly secure and as an adult becomes profligate and irresponsible.
- The child whose life was so insecure that as an adult she clings desperately to financial security.
- The child who was smothered and as an adult becomes a gambler to prove he is "bad".
- The divorcee who loses out financially and holds a perpetual chip on his shoulder against money.
- The young man who "sells his soul" for a promotion and forever wonders: "What if" ....
- The child who is "babied" and overly protected and as an adult is unable to take care of financial matters with assertiveness.

The list is as long as there are people.

But the good news is that once our patterns, our script, is revealed we are better equipped to recognize it and consider other choices.

As a financial planner part of my job was to help people establish their goals and always, not far into this process these questions would naturally arise:

"How much is Enough? How much do I need to feel secure?"

"How much would it take for me not to worry about money ever again?"

And whatever calculations and strategies I employed to come up with a number, the primary work had to start with self-knowledge and knowledge of their money script. There is no one size fits all. There is no one way for all to feel they have enough.

So, in order to start this process, I developed a quick and revealing question to ask at initial interviews in which clients instantly revealed their money script.

This question helps people see that there may be a disconnect between their script, their desires, and their reality. Try it.

If you had to identify yourself as one of the following money types, which are you?

The bag lady/bag man. This is you if you are deeply insecure around money and seriously believe there is a chance you will end up destitute and on the streets. Spending money is a painful process for you.

The Prince/Princess. This is you if you truly believe you will always have plenty, that if you run out, it will simply be replaced and there is no greater joy to you than spending money on the very best. It is your right!

The Ostrich. This is you if you have your head in the sand! It is you if you are not aware of your financial situation and you make no effort to find out about it. Bills often pile up as you are basically in denial about their contents.

My experience was that people always knew exactly which they were, and we would often chuckle at how decisions they wanted to make were based on this identity rather than their actual financial circumstances. By identifying their script, they were then able to contemplate life decisions based on what they really wanted from life and their actual financial situation, rather than a habitual story!

Another way to reveal your money script is to complete the sentence below. It will not be your full script, but it will be a clue.

If I let myself, _____, then _____.

When I did this years ago, I wrote, "If I let myself spend, then I will never stop".

The result of this fear was that I was unable to enjoy spending money, and this of course had a dangerously limiting effect on my experience of life. Once we recognize our deep-rooted beliefs, we can learn to smile at them and trust in our ability to moderate them if necessary.

Only by identifying your money script will you be able to take it into account and give your imaginations freedom to create the life you desire. And only then will you be able to use your resources efficiently to facilitate those ideas.

Self-Worth and spending?

As you make changes in your life you will probably need to look at your spending patterns, so it is imperative to look at how you react emotionally to it. Starting a business, for example, may take a big financial outlay with no guaranteed results.

Other changes may involve spending on travel, equipment, education, the possibilities are endless. How do you feel when you spend? Conversely, change may require that we severely restrict our spending for a while. How do you feel about *not* spending?

The way we spend may even reflect how we value ourselves, our sense of self-worth. As always, our primary tool for this exercise is our Witness. Looking at how we buy food is an easy example.

Do you always choose the cheapest item on the menu?

Does it cause you pain to see people wasting food?

Do you eat everything on your plate even when you've had enough in order not to be wasteful?

Do you always buy the same things at the store each week?

Do you always buy what's on sale? BOGO?

Do you buy what inspires and excites you?

How we spend is a direct inroad to our psychology...our ego...into our feelings of self-worth. We can learn so much about our money selves just by observing ourselves during a trip to the supermarket for a regular family meal!

Now let's broaden our inquiry by observing ourselves further during the process of spending in general. Here are some questions to consider about your spending behavior:

Do you feel real pleasure or guilt when you spend money?

Do you need to have the best to feel good about yourself?

Do you ever find yourself spending in order to impress others?

Do you ever boast about the amount you spent on a new purchase?

Do you boast about the "cheap deals" you found?

Are you a secret spender?

Do you only buy "on sale"?

Do you spend/give in order to receive love?

Do you spend in order to "keep up with the Joneses"?

Do you spend to compensate when something goes wrong?

Do you deprive yourself when something goes wrong?

What kind of event can cause either of the last two?

Are you totally honest with your partner about your spending?

Do you deny yourself what you want?

When do you treat yourself?

Do you suffer anxiety when you make a big purchase?

I know my first reaction to many of these questions was vehement. Please take a second look at them all, especially those you deny or accept vehemently and look a little deeper. If something is painful to acknowledge, don't judge or blame yourself, but be grateful for the heightened awareness. You now have an opportunity to redress the balance if you so desire.

There are many more questions that may come up, particularly if you do this with a partner.

Take a moment here and complete this statement from what you have learned.

Write it.

As a spender, I_____. (Continue to write until you have the full picture.)

How do you Feel about money?

This inquiry is short and sharp but revealing. Holding the idea of money front and center, look at the following list of emotions. Which ones are dominant for you? Notice that some are freeing and some cause compensatory behavior.

Circle any that resonate with you:

Fear

Competition

Guilt

- Greed
- Shame
- Regret
- Desire
- Envy
- Anxiety
- Pleasure
- Excitement
- Fun
- Satisfaction
- Gratitude
- Creativity
- Control
- Pride
- Energized
- Exhaustion
- Generous
- Responsible
- Balanced
- Tight
- Power

Add your own words. Review the ones you have circled. Is there a theme?

And finally, we have a conversation with money…

Conversation with Money

I invite you to try one last exercise and to take as long as you need to complete it.

Ask someone with whom you are close to help with this. All they have to do is sit with you, ***in silence***, pretending to inhabit the role of money. You then sit opposite them and have a conversation (one sided) with "Money" telling "Money" exactly how you feel about it and describing your relationship. Use the pronouns "I" and "You".

Once upon a time my conversation with Money started like this:

"I honestly believe I don't deserve you. I believe I will never have enough of you. I will always feel as if no matter what I do you will run away from me…." etc.

It is very powerful having someone playing the part of Money and speaking directly to them. It seems easier to describe your relationship, your fears, and aspirations when Money is personalized. I have known people talk to Money for half an hour or more and still feel they have more to say. It is often interesting to find out just how much you do feel about Money once you get started and just how freeing it is to express it all out loud.

Maybe at the end you'll even be able to lean over and give Money a big hug!

Hopefully, now you have a good insight into who you are as a money person. You know your strengths, weaknesses, your vulnerability and your power. You understand how money affects your self-esteem, your feeling of well-being, and how it drives so many of the decisions you make.

At this point, take some time to reconnect with Chapters 2 and 3 in which you took a deep look at your life, and what you need to feel whole.

Put that awareness together with what you have learned about your relationship with money and allow the picture to unfold.

Next, we turn to the "nuts and bolts" of money and a few essential facts and figures that may help you with creative solutions to financial issues as they occur.

And at each stage of the way we will continue to watch as we reinforce the connection between your money and your soul.

Chapter 5 - *Your Financial Picture*

With an understanding of money's emotional charge, and the challenge it presents to the desires of your soul, we turn now to the practicalities of money. We explore how to enlist money as your ally as you create the life you want. I will show you how to pick optimal financial strategies to pursue your life and remain at peace with money.

There are three equally important chapters in this section:

- The first helps you understand your current personal financial situation.
- The second describes the financial systems in our culture.
- The third explains the complex issue of investing.

For some of us delving into our finances is a delight and even a hobby. Others, the Ostriches in the previous chapter, find it intimidating and avoid it at all costs. But the cost is great. You risk not ever really knowing if the changes you anticipate in life are possible.

Whether you are in a partnership or single, it is imperative that all parties become intimately familiar with their financial details. If you are in a partnership, talk openly and honestly about your total financial situation, including all of life's tasks and the value you place on those. Decide if the job of financial housekeeping will be shared or one person's responsibility.

To assess your financial situation, you will create a working budget and a Net Worth statement. You will need to gather as much information about your finances as possible. Make sure it is all in order so you can see what is working, and what is not.

If you are confident that you already do this, review all your documents to make sure you're not missing anything. Whatever happens to your life plans, this process will stand you in good stead, and hopefully alleviate financial anxiety. Usually knowing how things are (even if not as good as expected) is better than imagining the worst!

Secondly, we'll turn attention to the financial systems that operate here in the United States.

Most of us find ourselves involved with financial systems of one kind or another, even if only a checking account, so better armed with a basis of understanding. Money can be your best ally, helping you transform not only your life but the lives of those you love and potentially the lives of many others.

Or it can be your worst enemy. Understanding how money works can save you from both counterproductive financial missteps, and unnecessary anxiety. Even a little knowledge can greatly alleviate anxiety and increase your ability to "stay the course" whatever your course may be.

The alternative, after all, is to avoid money altogether or hide it under the bed and watch it dwindle with inflation, get stolen, or destroyed in a natural disaster!

Finally, we'll look at the complex and emotional world of investing.

Admittedly it is easy to become confused, cynical, and disillusioned, bombasted as we are by the daily drama of the financial news. One day everything is great, the next the world is ending. Financial statistics reveal however, that although *stock* market moves can be fast and precipitous, economic cycles are usually slow, long, and somewhat predictable. And whereas the stock market can appear to be the *only* financial tool if you watch the news, in fact, it is but one of many.

So, your study here will not be of the day's hysterical headlines but of facts and figures with the hope that the more you know, the more your emotional reactivity can soften. Eventually, no matter what the economic news that day, you will maintain your equilibrium and not panic into making totally counterproductive decisions. You can learn not to respond with charged emotion but with logic, calm, and reassurance that your own money is situated appropriately for your age and goals.

Often, when the emotional reality of an investment plan arises, the plan gets sabotaged. A plan that, at the outset, seemed exciting and inspiring may gradually morph into a plan that seems irresponsible and reckless with the unpredictability of investing.

Easy to retreat then from your dreams and allow them to dissolve, as life returns to "normal".

This need not be the case. By using creative appropriate strategies, I hope you will see a way to create the life *and* the financial situation you desire.

Be sure, as you consider the ideas presented here, to take account of how they work for *you*, both financially and emotionally.

Your financial situation

1. Budget

As you start to work on your budget, take time to frequently revisit your "Life-Force": remember what you need to make your heart sing, remember how it feels when your soul is smiling. Keep that alive to maintain balance as you work on the finances. It is your work here always to find a way to unite your dreams with your finances.

I use the term "Budget" to mean the difference between the amount of money that comes into your household (income) versus the amount that leaves (expenses). This is different from the budget you will create specifically for new plans, be it a vacation or a new business.

Whether or not you end each month and year with more money coming in than going out, you need to know. Only then will you be able to make the necessary adjustments to facilitate your plans.

And it may surprise you to see that sometimes it even makes sense to have a negative budget. One period in my life exemplifies this…

As young adults my partner and I dreamt of buying a dilapidated old house and restoring it. We had no money.

We borrowed almost 100% of the cost of the house. We also borrowed all the money to renovate it. At the time we had 2 small children and no other income. Each month our living expenses were simply added to our debt. (We had at the outset spent much time with the bank manager explaining the plan and sharing the business plan). Eventually, after much sweat equity, the property was complete and was sold for a good profit. The bank was repaid but the profits immediately sunk into the next project. For several years our monthly budget was a very negative number as we built our net worth.

(Several caveats: this business plan works best in a rising real-estate environment and secondly you need a friendly bank manager with whom you share all the details of the plan with total disclosure. You need high risk tolerance and a lot of luck. Finally, even though the budget number was negative each month and year, we kept a monthly record of the ever-growing debt so we would not go over our total project expense goal.)

But to resume: Your budget may be recorded in whichever way is most efficient for you: computer spreadsheet, online budget calculator (Mint, Quicken, Schwab), smartphone, notebook, back of an envelope. Make sure however that you can compare month by month *and* year by year. Ensure it is easily accessible, and don't lose it!

When analyzing your budget, it is easy to become obsessive about every detail and in the end get frustrated, so remember that it is more important to complete the process, albeit less than 100% accurate, than not finish it or not do it at all. It is useful to keep a monthly budget but also essential to keep an annual one as income can arrive erratically throughout the year. Start with income.

Your income

Although a computer program can keep records and analyze your budget from whatever point of view you desire, you must first collect and input that data!

Gather the information about each source of income you have and make sure you check throughout the entire year. For instance, in my example above, we only got "paid" once every year or two, or sometimes less frequently!

If you are self-employed or your work consists of projects, your pay may be erratic. Often bonds and other types of securities pay dividends or interest quarterly, semiannually, or annually. Royalty checks and rent may also fluctuate. Winnings may be once a lifetime, tax refunds once a year! So, in order to capture every payment that comes your way, check thoroughly, then total for each month, and then total for the year.

Go through all statements of all the institutions into which you deposit money (or have it deposited).

a. Salary and wages should be recorded on your budget as "net" amounts. ("Net" means the amount you receive after all deductions are withheld.)

b. All other income, (rent, royalties etc) should be recorded as "gross" income on your budget. "Gross" income is the amount you receive before tax is paid.) Tax you owe on gross income will be recorded as an expense on your budget.

Make sure you record ALL sources of income, even those that have been paid to you in cash. Some of these will be taxable, some not. That discussion is outside our brief here but be sure and check with your tax advisor in order to determine what income may require taxation at year-end. Major sources of income include but are not limited to:

Salary, wages, pensions, annuities, business income, social security, capital gains, IRA distributions, rents, royalties, interest, dividends, gifts, inheritances, child support, alimony, insurance policy claims, sick pay benefits, workers' compensation payments, veteran's benefits, welfare, scholarships, and winnings.

When you have your total, put this number on one side of the ledger.

Your Expenses

I use my credit card for literally everything I possibly can, in order to accumulate "miles" for travel and sometimes for cash refunds. Then I import the credit card bills into a reliable computer program (I personally use Mint) and categorize the payments. That way I can see how much I spend each month and what I spend it on. For me, that is easier than carrying cash and possibly losing track of how the cash was used. Also, this allows you to create a chart of how you spend, which makes comparing each month and year relatively easy.

If you do enjoy withdrawing cash each week or month to have some readily available, just note that amount and categorize it as "miscellaneous expenses" or whatever best describes in general terms, how that money is used.

Regular monthly expenses may include the following:

Home related expenses: mortgage, rent, food, household expenses including repairs, child related expenses, debt obligations, healthcare expenses, transportation expenses, clothing, entertainment, pet related expenses.

However, as you work with an annual budget you will need to include some or all the following:

auto registration fees, car/home/life insurance, car/home maintenance, gifts, holiday events, pets, healthcare, and licenses, union dues, club memberships, professional licensing dues, memberships: museums zoos YMCA etc., tax preparation fees, income taxes, vacations, magazine/newspaper subscriptions, subscriptions to on-line streaming media, property tax.

Online budget and expense calculators are plentiful and include quicken.com and schwabmoneywise.com.

and Mint.Intuit.com. They will step you through the process, import information from your banks and investment companies and record and categorize your expense payments as they occur.

When you have the "expense" number for the other side of the ledger, you will be able to compare your total monthly/annual income to your total monthly/annual expenses.

So, do you make more than you spend? Is the income side of the ledger larger than the expense? Or vice versa? Do you have more or less at the end of each month? Is this intentional? Were you aware of it? How do you feel about that?

Most importantly, how does this current scenario fit with your future plans? Don't try right now to figure that out. Just be grateful that you now have a clear picture of your income and expenses from which to start the planning process.

These numbers will enable you to assess the amount of income that is most desirable for you and the minimum amount you need to "survive" .... should that be required for a period.

2. Your Net Worth

Your net worth is a snapshot of your assets, minus your liabilities (debts) taken at specific and regular points in time each year.

Once you have gathered all your information and created your Net Worth statement it is then easy to see your overall financial situation immediately. If you are making changes in life, it is essential to know where your assets are, and how they could be re-configured, if necessary, to achieve your new plans.

It is also useful to keep track of changing values and allocations so that there are no shocks when you come to implement your plans.

There are several issues to bear in mind as you track your net worth:

The Effect of Economic Cycles on your Net Worth.

Your net worth may trend up or down depending on what you own. If you own assets, such as stocks, whose values fluctuate dramatically, you may see frequent and unnerving swings in your net worth, particularly during periods of economic downturn.

Economic cycles and fluctuations are a fact of life. They may appear unpredictable as their frequency and duration vary. We will discuss later how to love them as well as fear them and see the opportunities they may present. Depending on your objectives, it may be psychologically challenging if a downturn hits soon after you start keeping a record of your net worth and at the first check, you find it has declined.

However, as your time horizon lengthens and you compare the current number with that of five or ten years previously, then the chances of an upward trend increase (unless you simply spent all your assets). Try very hard not to be disheartened by a downturn and do not make decisions in a panic that reverse your objectives.

The Effect of Inflation on your Net Worth

If you own property or shares of the stock of a company, the chances are, that over time, the value of these assets (and your Net Worth) will rise.

The economy occasionally enters periods of deflation or stagflation (high inflation combined with high unemployment and little demand) but generally, since economic records have been kept, inflation has averaged approximately 2.4% per year. When paying attention to all things financial we must assume that costs will increase by an average of at least that amount over time. In other words, the value of our assets (and money) will decline if they don't increase by at least 2.4% (on average) per year. In 1970 a quart of milk cost 20c!

For this reason, it is wise not to feel too pleased with yourself if your net worth remains static over time because in fact, it is declining by approximately 2.4% (or whatever the prevailing rate of inflation is), in real value per year.

As you develop your plans and goals and decide how to allocate your funds, it is useful to research the amount by which certain assets have inflated historically compared to others, and those which decline in value like cars, boats, planes etc. If you are saving for something that typically rises in price with inflation, a house or travel for example, your savings must also be rising in value, or you will never reach your goal!

Homeownership as a part of Net Worth

When calculating net worth for a specific future goal you must decide whether to include the value of your home if you own, or are in the process, of owning one. If you live in the house you are buying, then it may not be wise to include it in your net worth.

If, however, you plan to use your home to fund future plans (as will be described in Chapter 6), it may be valid to include it in your net worth calculations. For instance, you may plan to sell your home and realize the capital to use for future plans. Of course, this is only viable if the home you plan to move into costs less than the one you plan to sell!

Start your Net Worth report

As mentioned, there are many online Budget/Net Worth calculators. Explore several before choosing the one that suits you best. I use Mint.com which can update the value of my assets daily. Make a note of which one you are using and when you start.

Then decide how often you will check your net worth statement. Usually, it is fine to do this once or twice a year, but if you use an online calculator, it is very easy to do it more frequently if you wish. Remember though, it can be detrimental to check too often and want to change things too often, in the hope of making an improvement. This can be when poor decisions are made.

If you are doing it annually, mark your calendar right away with next year's date.

In the interim, be sure that if you make changes to any of your assets, you adjust your net worth report.

You should include all assets that have value or can be converted into cash. This of course is subjective so be realistic with things like furniture (and certainly TVs), some of which have very little resale value.

Here is a list of assets that can be included:

Cash, real-estate, land, bank accounts, investment accounts, rights/copyrights, loans/trust deeds, businesses/inventory, machinery, cars/vehicles, art, jewelry, furniture with resale value, enforceable claims against others, accounts receivable, variable annuities, patents/trademarks.

And liabilities:

mortgages, car loans, personal loans, or other debt.

Once you have entered all your information you will have an accurate picture of your net worth. From this information you can create a working budget for a particular project and track your spending.

With a good idea of your overall financial situation, you can start to look at financial strategies that will help you transform nascent dreams into reality. You can move forward with peace of mind and confidence.

Chapter 6 - *Financial Strategies*

Nearly all change involves some adjustment to existing financial situations. Meeting those adjustments head on can be the time when anxiety sabotages the plans.

Being aware of that is half the solution. Notice when anxiety arises, take a moment to breathe, and use some of the calming tactics we discussed before. And remember, small steps are fine.

As you consider the ideas in this chapter, pay close attention to your emotional reactions to them. Watch for feelings of fear and insecurity, pay close attention to them, and try to stay open to everything, at least initially. Ultimately you will design a plan that leads you in the right direction without stress.

When faced with life transitions, with turns in the road, it is understandable that initially, we meet internal resistance:

I can't afford that

That's not responsible

We may lose everything

I'll never be able to retire

What about the kids' education?

At times like this it is useful to remember the adage: "Never let money be a reason *not* to do" and persevere in finding solutions you can live with. Learn to use the resources available to you to sculpt a plan that is emotionally and practically sustainable.

Whether this section is a review for you or brand-new information, pick from it what you need. For the time being I am *excluding* investing from these strategies. I have dedicated the following chapter exclusively to "investing", partly because it is a complex subject, and partly because investing is generally appropriate for very specific and longer-term projects.

The topics I cover in this chapter are saving, working, borrowing, lending, trading, leasing, and begging!

Think of each strategy as a tool in your toolbox. You are in charge of it, not vice versa, and you will select the appropriate tool for each project. Although there is nothing new or revolutionary about any of these strategies, it is in the details of each that you will find the combination that can work for you.

Strategy #1. Save

The simplest way to accumulate money for change is to save! It may not always be the most appropriate strategy, but it can be low stress.

Let us first establish what savings are *not*. Savings are not investments. Depending on prevailing interest rates, they may not earn much interest. The principal value will not grow unless you compound the interest by adding it to principal each time it is paid. Even so, when interest rates are low, your savings may not even keep pace with inflation. In other words, over time the buying power of your savings may decrease. But apart from this "inflation risk", a savings account is a risk-free way to accumulate liquid cash.

So, what *are* savings? We save money with the main goal of preserving it. It should be available at any time you need it. It is liquid (immediately available), and its value is known. Period. It is a nest egg, a security blanket, an emergency fund, or funds for a near-term project. Usually, it is recommended to have about 6 months of total living expenses in savings in case of emergencies, but when life changes are being made you may decide to simply "save" for your plans with no risk. This will depend on the nature of your plan.

If you can commit your money for a longer period, it may be wise to invest in certificates of deposit (CDs) as they may pay slightly higher interest and are insured by the FDIC (Federal Deposit Insurance Corporation). But CDs are not liquid, the money is committed for a stated period, and there will probably be a penalty to withdraw it early. But if you are saving a specific amount to fund a project at a specific date you may be able to use CDs and tie the money up until it is needed in order to (possibly) make a little more interest. (Usually, the longer the time period that you commit your money for, the more interest you earn, but this is not always the case.)

So, if an integral part of your plan is to save either for emergencies or to fund a near term project, research a bank that you trust and does not charge fees on savings accounts. Then decide how much you need to save and how frequently that will happen. There are many institutions that offer savings accounts. The usual ones are regular bricks-and-mortar banks, investment firms, and online savings accounts. There are many issues to consider when choosing one that best suits your needs:

- APY (annual percentage yield). This is the interest rate you are paid. Per month interest is the quoted annual rate / 12, x the amount of savings you have.
- How often the rate changes. Sometimes banks offer "teaser" rates to get your business, then drop the rate. Also, rates may be variable and need to be watched.
- Is there a minimum deposit requirement?
- Is there a minimum balance requirement or a maximum balance limit?
- What are the withdrawal options? Is there a penalty for early withdrawal?
- Is your money insured? Up to what amount?
- Are there any fees?

Many of these issues are discussed at bankrate.com and it soon becomes clear that the highest APY is not the only criteria to guide your search.

There are many ways to get started with saving. Often the choice boils down to making more money and saving some. Or spending less so you can save. Here it will be useful to consult your budget to see if there are any non-essential expenses that could be cut, and the money saved. Do you really need those subscriptions? When did you last go to the YMCA?

These decisions, as most, are not just practical but emotional, and it is vital to decide on a savings figure that allows you to sleep at night and allows you to move ahead happily with your plan.

Find the savings plan that works for you, and you are more likely to stick to it. Here are some ideas:

- Exercise "domestic austerity" for a while by trimming the budget. These are times of rice and beans, not steak and caviar. Subscriptions are cut, eating out becomes eating in, coffee dates become walks. Decide on the amount you need to save each month and deposit it, religiously, into a savings account.
- Make austerity creative and fun. Unless austerity is fun it probably won't happen. So, invest in an austerity cookbook, buy better quality coffee so you save coffee shop dollars, have potlucks instead of extravagant dinners, buy candles and have romantic dinners at home, not out. Walk or cycle, don't drive, where possible. And then there's the creativity of thrift shops! Never forget, it's only temporary: - unless it's all too much fun.
- Label a jar with the title of your project. Each time you have any extra cash, put it in the jar. This works best for small projects like a trip.
- Deposit a predetermined percentage of your paycheck directly into a savings account on a regular basis.
- Earn more and save the extra. This could involve taking a temporary second job or evening work from home and saving every penny.

- If you are currently saving for long term goals such as retirement, education, a home etc. and putting various sums of money towards those savings on a regular basis you may be able to consider redirecting some of those funds towards your current project for a prescribed, limited period. If you need help, ask a professional to calculate how much you need to save, and for what period, to achieve the other time-specific goals. It may be possible to save less on some or all of them for a while. You may be more on track to meet your goals than you thought. Be very careful with these calculations, and very honest with anyone else they affect.
- In order to save for a specific project, ask for all gifts to be given as cash and save every penny in a separate account. Tell the gift givers about your idea and keep them updated with your progress.

And remember, saving is not investing. Investments may not be available when you need them. Savings are available.

One last word on savings. This may sound strange to some, but it really does happen that people lose track of what they own. Part of my responsibility as a Planner was to encourage clients to go through every document, scrap of paper, old files etc. that they could. It was always remarkable how many came across old investment accounts, savings, or bank accounts, even pieces of real estate that they had forgotten.

Strategy #2 Work

In an ideal situation our work is our purpose. It is not only a source of income but our creativity, our passion, the highest expression of who we are.

On another level work is merely a way to be recompensed for your labor. You give your time, and you get money!

For some of us passion and work are one and the same. For others, not so much.

What is work for you at the moment? Is it only a means of making money or would you do it even if you were not paid? Are you really alive when you are at work, or do you come alive when you leave and do something else?

If you spend the majority of your waking hours at work and it is simply a way to make a living, then the nature of your work may be the very thing that needs to change. Or, work may become part of a strategy to make other things happen.

Whichever your situation, consider these different scenarios, and whether any of them could either improve your current situation or help you move towards the change you seek.

- Consider work as primarily a means to earn money in the shortest possible time in order to fund a period of transition, or a change. Figure out how long this period needs to be and keep in mind that it is not an end in itself, but a pathway to the next chapter. Earn as much as you can as quickly as you can. Simultaneously start to research your new plans, gather information, and prepare to move ahead. This keeps life spicy and means you will be well prepared when the time is right, and the funds are available to make the change.

- Some of us enjoy the continuity of one lifelong career and enjoy "climbing the ladder" to increasing success and compensation. Others of us find this predictable and stultifying. If you fall into the latter camp, try considering work as a series of quite different chapters in which you explore different opportunities as they grab your attention. Allow the work you do to express and honor your personal evolution. The challenge is to know when one chapter is ending and another calling, knowing when one has run its course, and be able to make a change. The change you crave may exist simply in another occupation. Look at the possibilities.

- Sometimes temporarily increasing the intensity of work can help fulfill other plans and lead to a new direction. My friend, Steve, is a teacher and desperately wanted to own a home but needed extra cash for his down payment. He took on two extra jobs in addition to classroom teaching, President of the Teacher's Union, and curriculum supervisor for a school year. This strategy was extremely intense for one year but enabled him to afford the down payment on his house. An unexpected result was that his improved resume enabled him to segue into a career in Administration that he loved. He achieved two goals with one plan.

- Consider other ways to change your work from within if it is less than inspiring, but your circumstances do not permit you to leave. As my friend Jane put it: "Don't get paralyzed by following your bliss, but never give up on your bliss". Her job involved a lot of mundane data entry and routine desk work, but she saw an opportunity to get involved with staff training which led to travel, training, and coaching which she loved. She stuck with the job that allowed her to provide for herself financially but made it her own. She found her bliss within a potentially dull, but lucrative situation.

- If the concept of a traditional job is really anathema to you, consider working towards living off "passive income". This requires building your assets until they can provide sufficient income. It may require a period of austerity or of temporary/part-time jobs, or both. We listed alternative sources of income when calculating a budget above: rent, dividends, and interest from investments, annuity payments, royalties, pensions, and payments on loans (notes) you have made. Once you have accumulated enough capital assets you then have most of your time at your disposal.

- If you own property (real estate, RVs, trucks etc.) you may be able to use it in various ways to provide income. It may be possible, for instance, to board horses or rent the land to people growing small amounts of lucrative crops. Some can convert part of their homes (or RVs) into Airbnb or VRBO rental spaces or rent space to people wanting to hold meetings or classes. If you have an empty garage or storage shed, you may simply be able to rent space to people who need storage. A friend of mine wanted to raise extra cash for travel and had room in her house to rent but hated the idea of sharing her home. So, she rented the extra space to a massage therapist who was there during the day (when my friend was at work)- but was gone by the time she returned home. Be sure and check with your insurance company before you embark on any of these ventures to make sure it doesn't affect your coverage.

- One of life's most challenging decisions is whether to be self-employed or employed. The choice between a guaranteed regular salary or the freedom of self-employment may seem insurmountable, so trying a period of each may help with the decision. If self-employment is your dream, start by thoroughly analyzing your skills and knowledge. Consider if any could become a money-generating part of your life. I know people who have started consulting, coaching, cooking, dog-walking, solving IT problems, writing, etc. which have all led to profitable enterprises. It may be that just one or two well-paying clients are sufficient to provide the income you need and free up time to follow other pursuits. Choose your clients carefully and treat them well!

- It may be possible to consider working abroad for a limited (or extended) period. This can work in your favor in several ways. You may be able to significantly increase your earning capacity overseas. Living expenses may be less overseas and if you own a home, you may be able to rent it while you are away, for additional income. For those of you concerned about their school-age children, I recommend a great read, "The Global Student" by Maya Frost. Not only did she and her husband find first-class education for their 4 high school daughters without cost, but Maya found a whole new path for herself as a result of uprooting.

We usually spend a lot of our life "at work", make sure it works for you.

Strategy #3. Borrow

"Neither a lender nor a borrower be" ….

Both borrowing and lending come with huge responsibility and the power to significantly impact and change your lifestyle. Signing a legally binding contract to borrow money suddenly puts access to sums of money into your hands. It also requires that from that moment on you are beholden to pay back that money (with interest) probably every month. And that affects how you spend your time; it affects the very shape of your days and may even keep you tied to a job you hate.

For some people, the idea of being in debt is truly abhorrent and their one financial goal is to be debt free. They see debt as being beholden to the bank, having a noose around the neck. Others see it as access to funds and the opportunity of "making money with other people's money", leveraging their assets. Many people of course are only able to purchase their home by borrowing in the form of a mortgage.

So, the first thing is to be clear about how you feel about getting into debt. Does it feel like a noose around your neck, limiting your possibilities or does it seem to open a vast range of otherwise impossible opportunities? Whether you borrow a few hundred dollars for a trip or hundreds of thousands to start a business, find your comfort zone with debt so it does not force you into a life that further distances you from your soul and from the change you need to make.

Borrowing money is a complex issue and always requires careful consideration of many issues, some listed below:

Why Borrow?

Some situations where it may make sense to borrow are:

- You want or need something now in order to move forward with plans
- You don't have enough money now, but you expect to have more money later to pay off a loan
- You expect to make more money with the money you borrow than you are paying in interest on your loan
- What you want/need is increasing in price at a faster rate than the cost of borrowing to buy it now

Age

It may be less advisable to borrow a large amount of money later in life when earning (and therefore repayment) potential is possibly less.

Interest Rates

Do not try to second guess when and how interest rates will change. Naturally, it is wonderful to lock in a low-interest rate, but interest rate changes are unpredictable so waiting for interest rates to *possibly* come down (if they are currently high) could mean the loss of your opportunity. Act now if you are ready!

However, if you need to borrow money in a rising interest rate environment, you may be anxious to borrow as quickly as possible before rates go up still more. But you should always carefully weigh the advantage of a *possibly* lower rate, with the risk of making a hasty decision. Be patient if you are not ready!

Your decision should be based on how prepared you are, not on your guesses about the direction of interest rates.

Decide whether you will negotiate a fixed or variable interest rate loan if you have a choice. If interest rates are low, it may be advisable to "lock in" a long-term, fixed-rate loan depending on your plans. The rate on a "variable" loan may be lower than a fixed rate loan but will rise and fall with the dictates of the Federal Reserve. This can come as a nasty shock if rates (and your payments) start rising rapidly.

Always shop for the best interest rate available. Negotiate. The Central Bank sets the "risk-free" or "prime" rate as a baseline for lending institutions that add their percentage. But remember, the cheapest rate is not always the best. Read the small print and the conditions.

Repaying the Loan

A repayment plan is highly advisable in almost any situation if you are to negotiate a favorable agreement. Decide on the period of the loan and create a detailed, thorough, written repayment plan. If you are borrowing money for a business this will be required, together with your business plan.

In the case of a private loan both parties have a notarized promissory note kept in a safe.

The lender, be it a private individual or an institution, is hoping to make interest on the loan, or receive equity in your business, and in order to do so the lender is being parted from his money by lending it to you. You, and your ability and likelihood to repay the loan, are his risk factors. The more you can do, the more information you can give to help him feel you are a "safe bet", the better. Stick to your commitment impeccably and he will be more than happy to lend to you again. A good relationship between lender and borrower (whichever you are) is an invaluable tool in your financial toolbox.

Security

The lending institution that offers you a loan will require "security" for the money they lend you. This means that if you default on your loan the lender can take whatever you have pledged as Security. Security is also known as Collateral.

In the case of a real estate mortgage, the Security is the real estate you are buying. The same applies if you are buying a car, boat etc.

Other times the Security may be yourself, your reputation as a borrower, your ability (income) to repay the loan, or some other assets you own.

Types of Loan

There is a plethora of different loans, each appropriate for different projects.

Possible loan sources are:

Loans from yourself; home equity lines of credit, your Qualified Retirement Plan, your Roth IRA, and your Whole Life Insurance Policy.

Loans from friends and family, (which may be amortized or interest only)

Loans from future inheritances.

Loans from banks and credit unions; personal loans, business loans and overdrafts.

Loans negotiated by mortgage brokers, including reverse mortgages

Loans from private investors.

Loans from the Small Business Administration (SBA).

Margin loans from a brokerage account.

Venture Capitalists.

Angel Investors.

Loans from yourself.

If you own a home, a Roth IRA, a Retirement Account, or Life Insurance Policy you may be able to access the money (or equity) you have accumulated, in certain circumstances.

Having "equity" in an asset (often real-estate) means that the asset may be worth more (if sold today) than any loans or mortgages you already have against it. For example, if you own a house that could sell for $200,000 today and you owe $100,000 on it, you have 50% equity in it or $100,000 that would be yours if you sold the house and repaid the bank your loan of $100,000.

If you don't want to sell the house, you can potentially access some of that for your project by taking a Home Equity Line of Credit. But there are downsides to this strategy to be aware of. If real-estate prices are dropping, your $100,000 equity is becoming less and less even though you still owe the full $100,000 original mortgage you borrowed from the bank. And this is what happened in 2007/8. The housing bubble burst, prices dropped, and people found they owed more on their property than it was worth. Many people lost their homes by walking away from the loans. Their "equity" had evaporated.

If you do "borrow" from your equity in your home on a Home Equity Line of Credit (HELOC), interest rates charged on Equity Lines are "variable". This means they will rise and fall as the Federal Reserve decides to raise and lower the Federal Funds Rate. The highest it has been was 20% in 1979 and the lowest is 0.25 in 2008. Clearly these fluctuations will impact your monthly repayments.

Sometimes loans are tax deductible. Be sure to discuss any lending proposition with your tax advisor before proceeding.

Another potential way to borrow from yourself is to borrow from your Retirement Savings Account. Before doing this, it is imperative to discuss the conditions and advisability (or not) with a Financial Planner. If any money is "borrowed" from a tax deferred retirement account (IRAs, 401ks etc.) strict rules apply, with penalties and taxes to pay if not adhered to.

You can withdraw **contributions** you made to your Roth IRA anytime, tax- and penalty-free. However, if you withdraw any **gains,** you may have to pay taxes and penalties if you are under the age of 59½ and the account is less than five years old. You may be able to avoid penalties (but not taxes) in the following situations:

- You use the withdrawal (up to a $10,000 lifetime maximum) to pay for a first-time home purchase.
- You use the withdrawal to pay for qualified education expenses.
- The distribution is made in substantially equal periodic payments.

- You use the withdrawal to pay for unreimbursed medical expenses or health insurance if you're unemployed.
- You're at least 59 ½ years of age.

As you see, borrowing from Retirement accounts is a complex issue even with "after tax" contributions. Again, it is imperative before taking this step to seek the advice of a Financial Planner and always think long and hard before withdrawing from Retirement savings as accumulating sufficient funds for retirement is challenging enough without taking withdrawals along the way.

If you own a Whole Life Insurance Policy, you may be able to borrow from it.

Borrowing from your life insurance policy can be a quick and easy way to get cash in hand when you need it.

You can only borrow against a permanent or whole life insurance policy.

Policy loans are borrowed against the death benefit, and the insurance company uses the policy as collateral for the loan.

Life insurance companies add interest to the balance, which accrues whether the loan is paid monthly or not.

Loans from Friends and Family

It may be possible to borrow from friends and family but of course where personal relationships are involved, it is extremely important to make sure that everyone understands all details of the loan and is happy with the arrangement. All the details should be recorded in a promissory note, signed by all parties. An important detail is to decide whether the borrower will pay just the interest amount as a periodic payment, or whether the principal will be amortized over the length of the loan and added to the periodic payments.

Borrow from future Inheritances

Under certain circumstances it may be possible to borrow from an inheritance that you know is coming your way. This is only possible if the current owner of the assets is 100% sure they will not need the money for their own care or enjoyment during the period of the loan. It is also imperative to inform all other beneficiaries of the inheritance and to adjust the Will or Trust to reflect the fact that the borrower will receive proportionally less in the case of death before the loan is repaid.

Loans from Banks or Credit Unions

There are two ways to arrange a loan through a bank or credit union: a regular loan or an overdraft (AKA "Line of Credit") on your account. The interest you pay and the amount of the loan for both an overdraft and a loan will be determined by your credit score. The advantage of the overdraft arrangement is that it is more flexible, there are no time constraints, no charge to pay it off in full. The disadvantage is that the interest rate charged will be higher than on a regular loan.

Mortgages/Reverse Mortgages - through Mortgage Brokers

It is common practice, when buying a home, to pay a mortgage broker to manage the process of applying for a mortgage. They will work with different lenders to find the best rate and terms for you.

A reverse mortgage is available to people who are over 62 years or older (sometimes 55 or older). It allows people who have equity in their home to access some of that equity without having to sell their home. They borrow the equity in their home either as a lump sum, a monthly payment, or as a line of credit. The loan (reverse mortgage) is repaid, plus interest, from the proceeds of the home if it is sold at death, or when the home is sold. There are initiation fees and other costs associated with taking a Reverse Mortgage. All this of course reduces the value of the assets you leave for your heirs, so much research is recommended to make sure it is an appropriate move.

Loans from private real-estate investors, "hard money lenders".

"Hard money" loans are used to purchase real estate if, for some reason, you can't qualify for a traditional loan. The advantage of this type of loan is that they are quick to arrange and can be arranged for short time periods. The downside is that the interest rates are usually very high. The loan is based on the quality of the property and the "loan to value", rather than the creditworthiness of the borrower. Loans may be arranged through individual investors via a Private Equity broker or Hard Money Funds" all of which can be researched on the Internet. Ask for references and do as much due diligence as you can before taking a loan in this way.

Loans from the Small Business Association.

The SBA works with lenders to provide loans to small businesses. The loans are usually provided by community development organizations. Interest rates are usually competitive and required down payments can be lower. No collateral is needed for some loans. These organizations also often provide many other useful services for small businesses.

Venture Capitalists/Angel Investors

A venture capitalist (VC) is a private equity investor that provides capital to companies exhibiting high growth potential in exchange for an equity stake (part ownership of your business). This could be funding startup ventures or supporting small companies that wish to expand but do not have access to the equity markets. These are the steps to take before contacting a VC:

- Create a detailed business plan.
- Create a target list of VCs that are a good fit for your company by researching venture capital firms that invest in companies like yours.

- Ensure the firm invests in the stage and level of funding that you seek and check out the firm's past deals.
- Consider the firm's location.
- Organize your list and reach out to your target VCs.

Angel investors are individuals who invest in new or small business ventures, providing capital for start-up or expansion. They typically have spare cash available and are looking for a higher rate of return than would be given by more traditional investments. An angel investor typically looks for a return of 25 percent or more. Equity financing is normally used by non-established businesses that do not have sufficient cash flow or collateral with which to secure business loans from financial institutions. Angel investors fill in the gap between the small-scale financing provided by family and friends and venture capitalists. Attracting Angel Investors is not always easy, but there are things you can do. First, consider whether angel investing is truly for you and your business.

The big advantage is that financing from angel investments is much less risky than debt financing. Unlike a loan, invested capital does not have to be paid back in the event of business failure. And most angel investors understand business and take a long-term view. Also, an angel investor is often looking for a personal opportunity as well as an investment.

The primary disadvantage of using angel investors is the loss of complete control of your business as the investor becomes a part-owner. Your angel investor will have a say in how the business is run and will also receive a portion of the profits when the business is sold. With debt financing, the lending institution has no control over the operations of your company and takes no share of the profits.

"Angel investor" is a somewhat general term, and you can find these types of investors in a few different forms. Angel investments normally come from wealthy individuals such as successful businesspeople, doctors, lawyers, and others that have a high net worth and are willing to invest up to (typically) $500,000 in return for equity (partial ownership of your business). Often this is done by word of mouth through business associates or associations such as the local Chamber of Commerce. Angels are increasingly operating as part of an angel syndicate (a group of angel investors), which raises their potential investment level accordingly. Investors contribute funds to the syndicate and a professional syndicate management team chooses the investments.

Whenever you are considering borrowing money, it is imperative to fully understand the ramifications of taking any loan and to seek independent, professional advice. This is vital in all cases but particularly if there is the possibility of penalties and fines, for instance, when borrowing from a Qualified Retirement Plan.

Strategy #4. Lending.

Lending is a strategy for those who have a large amount of cash and need an income stream. The simplest way to "lend" is to deposit money in a bank (lend it to the bank) and they will pay you interest. Alternatively, you can lend it to the government or a corporation as a "bond" and receive interest.

You can also become a private real estate lender as described above, either individually or as part of a fund. This type of lending will pay you higher interest than a savings account but is riskier. It requires considerable real-estate knowledge.

Strategy #5. Trading, leasing.

If your project requires you to buy something, be it a building, equipment, or materials, consider your options carefully. It's easy (and sometimes necessary) to spend money to buy, but if money is limited, it is worth considering alternatives.

Trading is one such alternative. There is often someone who needs a skill or "thing" that you have who may just have the skill or thing that you need.

An acquaintance of mine wanted to start a yoga studio, but the outlay to buy one was out of her reach. Instead, she networked until she was offered the perfect location for her first yoga retreat in exchange for free participation at the retreat and ongoing yoga instruction. As it turned out, the enterprise evolved in a way that did not require her to own a studio, so she saved both money, time, and effort by stepping lightly into her business.

If funds are short or if you want to see success before you invest, consider leasing before you buy. During my research I met vintners who leased land to grow grapes from landowners, who needed their acres cared for. Conversely, I met Doug who bought his boat by placing it in charter (leasing it to others) for several years in order to pay down the loan until it was manageable for him.

Do you have to buy new? Do you have the time/skills to make what you need instead of buying?

Would it be possible to borrow what you need or lease it?

Strategy #6. Begging

Explore programs like Kickstarter, Indiegogo, RocketHub, FundRazr, Pozible, Uele, Fundable, FundAnything, Quirky as potential ways to raise funds. Of course, these aren't strictly begging as these programs work by offering rewards to your donors, but they are all possible ways to raise seed money for your project.

Grant writing may become a skill to hone along with writing persuasive letters to companies or organizations asking for sponsorship. And as you ask, give. Offer something in return for their support.

Practice your powers of persuasion as you "sell" your idea to a wealthy friend or relative and always consider their needs and how you can make it an attractive proposition to them, so they too win through your endeavors.

Whichever strategy or strategies you choose to facilitate the change you seek, unleash your enthusiasm, and allow it to inspire whoever you work with.

Chapter 7 - *Investing*

Becoming a successful investor is one of life's greatest challenges, not because of choosing the best investments, but because of managing the psychological demands.

It is a serious, long-term endeavor.

It should both reflect your values, and help you achieve financial goals so you can be independent and responsible to yourself, your family and society. It is a baseline from which your dreams can take flight, knowing that your longer-term goals of retirement, a child's education, and long-term care, are being taken care of with your investments.

We will take a brief look at the whole process, from planning, the nature of risk, choosing accounts, asset allocation, diversification, rebalancing a portfolio, market cycles, and timing the market.

Successful investors don't focus on being with or against the crowd, they focus on their own goals and needs, their own assets, tolerance for risk, and timeframe. What other people do and what today's headline might be, has no impact on their investment decisions.

The problem is, when it comes to investing, it is only human to feel greedy for whatever is gaining in value and frightened of what is losing value. Learning to reverse those impulses and to buy what is "on-sale" and stay away from things that are overpriced, is one of the biggest challenges for investors.

The best option is to stick with the investments that are appropriate for your age and goals, monitor if they are still sound, and buy them when they are "on-sale

As Warren Buffet says: "You want to be greedy when others are fearful. You want to be fearful when others are greedy. It's that simple"

Try not to react emotionally to what you read or hear in the media and notice, with a smile, how the Financial Press headlines swing almost daily from despondency to exuberance.

To start, here is a simplified definition of the various asset classes and their basic distinguishing qualities.

1. **Types of Investment**

- Cash will only change in value by the amount of interest it earns, if you add the interest to your original amount. It will not earn as much as some other investments, but it will provide an anchor to a portfolio and will be available when you need it.
- Shares of "stock" are an actual share of a company that the company sells to you to fund their operation. Your investment rises and falls on the fortunes of the company. Shares of stock may also pay dividends. Many people prefer to buy "baskets" of stocks in the form of Mutual Funds or Exchange

Traded Funds. Over time a portfolio invested only in stocks will fluctuate considerably in value, both up and down. For instance, the markets took about 25 years to recover to pre-crisis values after the Great Depression, and about 4 years after the Recessions of 2000 and 2008. During the 2007-2009 Recession, the S&P 500 (an index of 500 companies) lost approximately 50% of its value.

- Bonds are loans. Investors lend a company (or the government) an amount of money and the company (or government) pays interest on the loan. At the end of a fixed period, the borrower hopefully repays the debt to the investor. Bonds may be bought individually or as mutual funds and ETFs (Exchange Traded Funds). Bonds do fluctuate in value, but usually not as much as stocks and if you keep a bond to maturity, you need not pay attention to these fluctuations. Bond mutual funds and ETFs do not have maturities and they will fluctuate in value so are not so suitable if you need the capital at a fixed date in the future. It is possible to compound the interest paid by mutual funds and ETFs by reinvesting the interest.

- Commodities. Commodities are raw materials, everything from soybeans and wheat to gold, silver, oil, and gas. There are several ways to consider investing in commodities. One is to purchase varying amounts of physical raw commodities, such as precious metal bullion. Investors can also invest in futures contracts or exchange-traded products (ETPs) that directly track a specific commodity index. These are highly volatile and complex investments that are generally recommended for sophisticated investors only. But depending on the size of your portfolio and your expertise, it may be appropriate to add a small percentage of a commodity-rich mutual fund or ETF for diversification.

- <u>Currencies</u>. Investing in currency involves buying the currency of one country while selling that of another. This is done through the foreign exchange market, or "forex." Once again this is a complex business requiring a lot of knowledge of the economy and political stability of the countries you are considering. Currency investing once again provides yet another level of diversification to a portfolio, but investors may find it easier to add an "International" mutual fund or ETF that invests in the stocks of bonds in the currency of that country.
- <u>Bitcoin and other cryptocurrencies</u> are also of increasing interest to the investing community. The value of these "currencies" is dependent on the faith of investors, its integration into financial markets, public interest in using it, and its performance compared to other investments. These currencies are highly speculative because although they are "currencies" and do resemble money is some ways, they are used for relatively few actual financial transactions.
- <u>Real Estate</u>. Real-estate may be purchased in the form of physical property such as apartments, offices, shopping malls etc. or as REITS. A Real Estate Investment Trust (REIT) is a company that owns, operates, or finances income-generating real estate. Modeled after mutual funds, REITs pool the capital of numerous investors. This makes it possible for individual investors to earn dividends from real

estate investments—without having to buy, manage, or finance any properties themselves.
- There are also mutual funds and ETFs that invest exclusively in REITs.

2. Planning

Make a list of your financial goals and their timeframes.

As we are looking at the long term, investing goals are usually: Retirement, financial independence, education for self and/or children and long-term care. But if you are a young adult and have goals for 10 - 20 years hence, it may be appropriate to invest for other goals such as starting a business, the down payment on a house, marketing an invention, extended travel, etc.

Your investment priorities may also need to be adjusted (either temporarily or permanently) as your life planning evolves.

Your goals and timeframe will be revised and revisited as circumstances change (a raise, inheritance, loss of job, birth of child, change of plans, etc.), but start with what you know now and write a plan. Seek professional help if you need it.

3. Risk

Just as you shouldn't undertake an expedition through the jungle without knowledge of the dangers you will face from the various creatures you will encounter, so it is essential to start any discussion about investing with an examination of the various risks associated with the different investments you are about to encounter. Just as every innocuous-looking little spider in the jungle may have a lethal sting, so every financial instrument (yes, even your checking account) comes with potential risk. With knowledge of these risks, we can choose investments appropriate to the goal we are trying to achieve and formulate a plan with eyes wide open.

I have known many people tempted to jettison their dreams because they have not understood the investments they chose and wanted to jump ship at the worst possible time. Better instead to be well prepared and able to stay the course. To meet your goal.

Let us dig a little deeper into the meaning of financial risk.

When it comes to money, risk basically means...losing it!

There are several ways to lose money completely. The first is to gamble. We put our money on the table, throw the dice and win or lose. Period.

The second way is to lend money to someone (or entity) that does not repay it. This could take the form of a private loan to someone to fund their project, or it could be investing in a bond (lending your money to a corporation or government). If the individual or entity goes bankrupt, there is a good chance that the principal amount of the loan will be lost, or reduced.

The third way of losing money completely is to sell an investment when its value is less than you paid for it. For example, if you buy 100 shares of stock at $10 a share, it will cost you $1,000. If you sell your 100 shares when they are valued at $5 per share you will have lost $500. In some situations, it may be advisable to cut losses in this way. But nevertheless, the $500 is lost. At other times it may be wise to double up on the investment and wait.

Here is a list of the most common risks associated with basic investment instruments:

Inflation Risk.

In the section on "saving", we described the risk inflation presents when we are saving for something that is rising in price with inflation faster than the money we are saving.

Here we look at the effect inflation has on specific investments, particularly bonds. There are three main ways inflation presents risk to bond investors.

The first is that the interest paid to you on bonds is a fixed payment, established when you buy the bond. It will not change over the duration of the bond, even if that is 30 years. This means that, with inflation, the purchasing power of those payments becomes less.

Secondly, when the economy is showing signs of inflation, the Federal Reserve is likely to raise interest rates. The interest rate on bonds you already own will not change and this means the value of your bonds will decline (bond buyers can buy better bonds that pay more than yours, so yours loses value). This is only a problem if you need to sell your bond before it matures (returns your principal), at the end of its term.

This brings us to the third problem with bond investing and inflation. If you buy a bond for $10,000 which lasts for ten years and there is 2% inflation each year for those ten years, the principal amount, when returned to you at the end of ten years, will be worth

20% less in real terms. So, you will have 20% less real value to reinvest.

Which brings us to:

Reinvestment Risk.

Reinvestment risk is the risk that when your capital is returned to you when a bond matures you will not be able to reinvest that capital at the same rate you have been receiving. This risk applies to CDs, Treasury, and corporate bonds. For instance, if you own a bond paying 6% interest in a falling interest environment and the capital you invested is paid back to you, you may only be able to reinvest it at 4% for an equivalent bond going forward. This will certainly affect how quickly you accumulate funds to meet your goal.

So, although bonds are generally less volatile than many other investments, they have other risks, due to inflation. This is why investors sometimes decide to diversify some of their portfolio to stocks and real estate, which tend, over time, to rise with inflation.

Interest Rate Risk

The Federal Reserve is a body that manages the nation's banking system and creates monetary policy. One of its many mandates is to adjust interest rates periodically based on their assessment of the health of the economy. This rise and fall in interest rates can affect planning in several ways and it is important to pay attention to them as we plan.

Interest rates provide a barometer of the overall health of the economy. The Federal Reserve will start to lower interest rates when it feels the economy is in trouble and it needs to stimulate it by making money "cheaper" to borrow and therefore more accessible for people and corporations to borrow.

The Federal Reserve will start to raise interest rates if they feel the economy is overheated and there is a danger of inflation due to too much demand for goods and services. By raising interest rates, they make it more expensive to borrow money, demand drops, and the economy starts to cool.

All this affects planning when either borrowing, buying, investing, or saving. In addition, interest rate movement affects the overall "mood" of the economy, be it pessimistic or optimistic and this, in turn, can affect how we "feel" about making plans. We have described above the effect on interest rate changes on bonds. A change in interest rates may also influence the Stock Market.

Stock market fluctuations are driven by a lot more than just the rise and fall of interest rates, but stock prices sometimes fall in times of high interest rates as investors recognize that they can possibly get better returns (higher interest payments), from bonds without taking as much risk as in the stock market.

Also, as the Federal Reserve is trying to cool the economy by raising interest rates, corporate growth may slow, having a negative effect on the Stock Market.

Credit Risk.

Credit risk is the risk that a company, person, or government you invest in may fail and not make the expected interest or dividend payments.

Companies are rated on a system from Aaa to C. There are three main ratings agencies that evaluate the credit worthiness of bonds: Moodys, Standard and Poor's, and Fitch. In general, bonds issued by companies with high ratings will pay less interest than those with a low rating.

This is the same system you will encounter if *you* apply to borrow money or take a mortgage. The lender will assess how risky you are and base the amount of money they lend and the interest rate they charge on the risk you present to them!

Liquidity Risk

Liquidity risk arises when you are unable to turn an asset into cash quickly and easily. For example, if you have an immediate need for cash (the perfect opportunity you have been waiting for arrives), but because the cash you need is tied up in assets that are hard to liquidate immediately, you may be forced to sell for a lower value. Common examples of this are real estate, real estate loan funds, CDs or other investments that have a penalty to sell before a named date in the future.

Capital Risk

Capital risk is the potential for loss of part or all your invested capital. It applies to any asset that is not subject to a guarantee of full return of original capital. Investors face capital risk when they invest in stocks, non-government bonds, real estate, commodities, currencies, and other alternative assets.

However, as indicated above, it is possible to some extent, to mitigate capital risk by assessing the quality of the issuer of your investment.

Personal tolerance for risk (fluctuation in value).

As you see above, each investment has its own risks. Unfortunately, the assets that *may* increase the most in value over time, may also be the most volatile (risky). It might seem logical therefore, for people who are risk averse, to avoid these volatile animals! But, depending on your goals and timeframe, it may be necessary to expose some percentage of a portfolio to them, simply to realize the goal. The question is: how much?

And the conundrum is:

With too much exposure to risky investments, investors will panic and sell them all in periods of extreme volatility and not achieve their goals.

Or, with too little exposure to risky investments, the goals may never be achieved!

So, it is imperative to establish as well as possible exactly how you react emotionally to the way each type of investment behaves. Only with this knowledge about yourself will you be able to pick investments that you can live with and stick to, investments that will help you stay the course and reach your goals.

The best way to do this is simply to Google "risk tolerance questionnaire". Many will come up. Look at several and choose the one that you can relate to most. I find the one offered by Vanguard to be thorough and helpful. It will help you understand how the different investment options behave and which ones, for your circumstances, are the most suitable.

After many years of guiding people through the journey of becoming successful investors, I know how hard it can be. With increased knowledge and experience it becomes easier to choose investments that give you peace of mind. Being able to stay the course, knowing how much volatility and fluctuation you can tolerate is a valuable and rare skill. Unless you are only investing in very low risk assets such as CDs and Treasury bonds, investing almost invariably requires a long-time horizon. The length of time depends on the type of investment, but if you are considering the stock market or real estate, you should in my opinion, be prepared to stay invested for at least 10 years.

And remember, the earlier you start, the more likely you are to catch the worm! Start investing as soon as you can and add to your investments on a regular basis throughout your life.

4.   Pick your Investment Account

One of the first things to do is decide what type of investment account you will start. There are three different types of investment accounts: currently taxable, tax-deferred, Roth accounts, and 529 college savings accounts.

If you are employed, your employer may offer a Retirement account that both he and you contribute to.

If you start your own business, you will have specific Retirement Plans available to you depending on the structure of your business. You will consult with your tax adviser about which one is best for you.

This is how they work:

- Currently taxable investment accounts or saving accounts are accounts that you fund with your after-tax money, and you pay tax on any interest, dividends, or gains you make each tax year.
- "Tax-deferred" accounts are Retirement accounts that you fund with income before it is taxed (IRAs, 401Ks, 403bs, SEP IRAs, Simple IRAs.) In other words, you may be able to take a tax deduction on your contributions to these accounts up to specific limits. You will pay tax on the full amount you withdraw. When you reach the age of 70 ½ the IRS requires that you start withdrawing from these accounts and there is a penalty for not doing so.
- Roth Retirement accounts are accounts that are funded with after-tax income (you get no deduction for your contributions), but the income and gains they make are tax-free. Here, briefly, are the rules for withdrawing money from a Roth IRA:

You can always withdraw the money you have contributed to a Roth without penalties or taxes.

You can withdraw contributions and earnings from a Roth if you are over 59 ½ and have held the account for at least 5, years without penalties and taxes.

Special exceptions are made for people under 59 ½, or who haven't held the account for 5 years, for first-time home purchase, college expenses, adoption costs etc.

- There are contribution limits on all retirement accounts. It is important to calculate whether to invest in either a Roth or Traditional Retirement account (or both), depending on your current and future expected tax bracket. It is also possible to convert Traditional Retirement accounts into Roth accounts by paying the tax owed. It will then continue to grow tax-free.

- 529 college savings accounts are designed to save specifically for post-High School education. They are funded with after-tax money, but in most states, a state tax deduction is available for contributions. Withdrawals from a 529 plan that are for strictly qualified education tax-free. "Target date" investment options are usually available in 529 plans in which you state the date that the funds will be needed. The investment company adjusts the asset allocation of the portfolio, so the money is available when needed.

Due to all these different tax implications, it is important to seek advice from a Financial Planner about how they all work, and which are suitable for you.

5. Asset Allocation

A portfolio's "Asset allocation" refers to the percentage of the investment capital that is invested in each asset class (stocks, bonds, etc..).

After deciding on the type(s) of account you will establish, asset allocation is the first thing you should consider when getting ready to create a portfolio because it has the most effect on the volatility (change in value) of your portfolio.

Before starting even the smallest investment program, become familiar with the potential volatility of each asset class you are considering and select only the amount of more volatile investments that you can tolerate in order to reach the goals you are pursuing.

By allocating your assets in this way you have a certain amount of control over the volatility of your overall portfolio.

With little or no knowledge of investing, people sometimes choose a strategy that is too risky because the upside looks so attractive. But when the markets then tumble dramatically the danger is that the inexperienced investor will abandon all the volatile investments, and replace them with ones that appear "safe" but may not enable goals to be reached. Better to start out with a plan that can be tolerated throughout the ups and downs of the time period you have set for yourself.

My advice, even if you are young, is to err on the side of safety because investing is one of the most challenging psychological and emotional activities there are. You can always increase your risk level as you gain experience and see how your investments behave.

As with everything else we are discussing, the more self-knowledge you have the better you will fare as you confront feelings of fear and greed. Make sure you are prepared emotionally for whatever course you choose.

One way to experience your own emotional reactions to investing is to create 3 practice (pretend) portfolios (one high risk, one moderate, and one low risk) and watch them every day to experience the volatility. This will give you a taste of how it might feel when real money is on the line. Monitor these 3 portfolios every day especially if there are big swings in prices. You can easily "invest" by choosing Exchange Traded Funds (ETFs) that reflect the whole stock or bond market. One portfolio could be 100% stocks, one a 50/50 split, and one 100% bonds. See how you feel as they fluctuate in value and monitor your comfort zone. Ask yourself how you would feel about adding to the investment that is going down (buying low) ...or selling some of the one that is going up (selling high). Become familiar with how you feel about the risk and reward of each portfolio.

Here is just one example of Asset Allocation, but finding the percentages that are right for you should be taken very seriously:

Cash: 10%
Stocks: 40% (10% International)
Bonds: 30%
Real Estate: 20%

There is no "best" asset allocation. Creating a portfolio depends on age, circumstance, goals, and tolerance for volatility. As we age it may be more likely that our investments become a source of income so usually at this time, we need to lessen the fluctuations in value (more bonds, less stock). The best way to decide on what is right for you is to consult a financial professional or work with a Risk Tolerance questionnaire.

6. Diversification.

With your type of accounts chosen, and your asset allocation decided, there is still more work to be done before you invest. You will now need to diversify within the asset classes. We do this to further manage the volatility of a portfolio. The idea is to pick a wide variety of investments that are not "correlated", in other words, that do not all rise and fall at the same time, for the same reasons.

Here are some suggestions of ways to diversify your assets:

Stocks can be diversified into small, medium, and large companies, growth and value stocks, and international and domestic companies. Growth stocks tend to sell for a high price compared to the earnings of the company. Value stocks sell for a price that reflects the current earnings of the company.

Bonds can be diversified into government, corporate, municipal, high-yield, and inflation-protected bonds, both domestic and international, that mature (return your principal) over different time periods.

The easiest way (particularly if your capital is limited) to invest in a broadly diversified portfolio is through mutual funds or ETFs (exchange-traded funds). These investments allow you to spread your money between the many types of stocks, bonds, and real estate.

Easier still and arguably the best way to achieve ultimate diversification if money is limited, is to invest in a variety of individual investment indices (for instance the S and P 500) or even "the total stock market" and "the total bond market". A "Total Stock/Bond Market" ETF is one that tracks an index that is based on virtually the entire stock/bond market of a country or region.

A portfolio's asset allocation and diversification are the major determinants of its risk-and-return characteristics.

7. **Re-balance**

Because asset classes behave differently over time, the portfolio's asset allocation will change without adding or taking from it, and need to be re-balanced. "Re-balancing" means reducing assets that have grown to a larger percentage of the portfolio than your original allocation and adding to assets that have declined in value and now occupy a smaller percentage than your intended allocation.

For example, imagine you selected an asset allocation of 50% stocks and 50% bonds 4 years ago. During this time stocks return an average of 8% a year and bonds 2%, and you find that your new asset mix is more like 56% stocks and 44% bonds. In this example, you are now overweight in stocks and underweight in bonds. You will need to sell some stock and add to your bond investment to bring your portfolio back into balance.

If you check your portfolio at least twice a year and your mix is off by at least 5 percentage points, consider rebalancing. If you don't re-balance, you'll end up with an asset mix that doesn't match your risk tolerance.

How often should an investor rebalance their portfolio considering that re-balancing will take time and possibly money? Re-balancing a portfolio can incur the cost of transactions and possibly taxes. Unless your circumstances change significantly, annual, or semiannual monitoring is likely to produce a reasonable balance between risk, control, and cost for most investors.

Annual rebalancing is likely to be preferred when taxes or substantial time/costs are involved.

If you invest in a taxable account, selling investments that have gained value will mean you'll owe taxes. To avoid this, you could rebalance only within your tax-advantaged (IRA or Roth, 401K, etc.).

It can be hard to convince yourself to rebalance. Selling "winning" investments probably goes against your instincts. But it reflects one of the simplest distillations of investing wisdom: "Buy low, sell high."

8. Market Cycles

A market cycle is the movement of increasing prices and strong performance, or bull market, through a period of weak performance and falling prices, or bear market, and back again to new strength.

Typically, it is said that we have entered a Bear Market when the indices have fallen 20% or more from their 52-week high and that it is over when prices have risen over 20% from the 52-week low.

The chart below shows how often from 1900 to 2016 the stock market fell, how far it fell, and for how long. It tells us a lot about the past but remember:

1. No one can predict consistently when market declines will happen.

2. No one can predict how long a decline will last.

3. No one can consistently predict the "best" time to get in or out of the market.

Type of Decline	Av. Frequency	Av. Length
-5% or more	About 3 times a year	47 days
-10% or more	About once a year	115 days
-15% or more	About every 2 years	215 days
-20% or more	About every 3.0 years	367 days

Normal bear market cycles are also known as cyclical bear markets. But unfortunately, there are also secular bear markets which are much longer term.

They last anywhere between 5 and 25 years, although the average length is around 17 years. During that time, normal bull and bear market cycles can occur.

A ferocious bear market can easily wipe out months or even years of hard-won gains made in a bull market. And that is why, as we've already strongly asserted, it is so important to be appropriately allocated, to take profits on a regular basis, and to have a long-term time horizon.

9. Trying to "Time the Market"

I fully understand just how hard it is to stay the course during these periods of stock market decline, especially the long ones when a year (or more) goes by and all we see, at least from our stocks, is loss. And so often the desire to "Time the Market" gets the better of even the most seasoned investor. Those who "time the Market" believe they know when the stock market has reached either a high or a low and they base investment decisions on these feelings. Often these decisions are in fact based on fear or greed!

Sometimes the pain of a falling market is too intense, and people jump ship, selling the entire portfolio.

At other times, the temptation is to jump ship when the market is high and fear of collapse arises.

After a steep decline "market timers" often sell at the button, then they buy back in, often after it has already recovered at least 20%.

In both situations a little re-balancing is probably all that is required. But often, when erratic markets make investors feel out of control, they grasp for control by predicting where the market is heading. This is of course the one thing that is impossible to know. Predicting market movements is indeed a fool's game. Making decisions based on where you "think" the market is going almost always results in a lower average return over time.

The truth is that if you miss the 5 biggest "up" days a year by trading in and out, you lose 20% of the potential gain for the year.

Hopefully, at this point, you have a good idea of your money psychology and the basics of Financial Planning. You are better prepared to consider some creative strategies that will move you, without fear, with enthusiasm, towards the realization of your next chapter.

The next section takes us through some in-depth planning processes.

Chapter 8 - *Important questions*

Let's connect all the dots! Think back to earlier chapters where you felt your heart sing! Remember how it felt when your soul came alive with a rush of energy. Rest assured that with the knowledge you now have about money, and how you deal with it, your dreams can be realized with financial, and emotional ease.

But before we bring it all together and work on the details, there are some important big-picture questions to contemplate. The big picture questions all involve the practicalities of life, and it is vital to answer them while holding close the three fundamental inquiries that weave through this whole process:

Who am I?

Why am I here?

Where am I going?

Unless we feel our truth in the answers to those questions, the rest of the work has no value.

So far you have been able to work through these chapters either as an individual, *or* with a partner. But for these big picture questions, if you have a partner (either romantic, business or both) it is vital to work through them both independently *and* together.

If you are single most of these questions are still just as important.

These are some of the questions that arise when we embark on any change in life. It may seem easier to look the other way and ignore them. Do that at your peril!

They are the foundation of any plan for change and must be addressed if you are to be clear about your way forward. Many of these questions involve money so be sure to keep everything you learned in the last three chapters at the front of your mind and heart.

Please make notes of your answers. And remember they are merely a snapshot of one moment in time. Your answers may change and evolve. It is fascinating to track this evolution. As you revisit the questions even in a few months' time, you may be surprised to see which of your answers have become reality and which ones need to be updated.

Answer truthfully now but don't attach to your answers, especially if you and your partner disagree. Stay flexible!

Once everyone is clear about these basic lifestyle issues, then you can experience the thrill of your plans taking flight, even if they are the merest tweak to the life you already love. Let's get started:

Work.

We have already looked at the many ways work can be used as a financial strategy. We now make the inquiry personal. Which of the following best describes the role you would like work to play in your life:

- A means of producing as much money as possible in the shortest possible time and being financially independent as soon as possible.
- Primarily a way to make money but must also be enjoyable. Intention to "retire" at the normal age, about 65.
- A way to express your unique skills, passion, and values. Being paid is merely a bonus. The intention is to "work" far into old age, health permitting.
- A way to leave the world a better place than you found it.
- Do you lean more towards self-employment or being employed? This is a fundamental decision and whether one or both partners anticipate self-employment, it is essential for both to be on board as income may become erratic and sporadic. Work hours may be unpredictable and long.

You may find your answers incorporate several of the options.

- By incorporating the ideas about work/earning outlined in Chapter 6, write a brief description of how your remaining years of work would best facilitate your most fulfilled life?
- How does it compare to your current work situation?

Income/money management

Ideally, how do you prefer to receive income? (Remember to consider the different taxation of each).

Weekly/monthly paycheck?

Income (possibly sporadic) from a business or enterprise?

Passive income from rents, royalties, or investments?

Sporadic income from completion of a project?

Other?

A combination of several/all the above?

How important is income to you? Do you need the minimum to get by? Do you enjoy a little extra disposable income? Do you thrive on having a lot more income than you need every month?

Which of the following do you long for **most** now?

More income to spend and enjoy now?

More income to save for an early and comfortable retirement?

More time to pursue your interests and move in a new direction?

More time for family and friends?

Consider how you feel about these money questions:

Do you believe that earning is a shared responsibility?

How do you divide all the tasks of daily life? Do you believe they are all equal value? Do you share your income(s) equally?

Is your money in joint accounts? Are you both happy with that?

If just one person is earning, where is the money deposited?

If one of you brought more assets (or inherited assets) to the partnership, are they now shared?

Do you have a prenuptial agreement if you are married?

Do you have a Living Together agreement if you are not married?

If you plan to have children or start a business or follow a pursuit that initially has no income, how do each of you feel about one or the other of you not earning money for a period? For how long?

Are you accountable to each for your individual spending?

Do you make money decisions separately, or do you share them?

What are the financial issues that you disagree about? Is this important to you? How do you deal with disagreements?

How do you delegate financial responsibilities and management? Who is the financial caretaker of the household? Do you see that changing as life changes? Does one person do it all? Who pays the bills? Who deals with the taxes? Who does the long-term planning/saving? Who budgets household expenses?

Do you argue about money? What about it? Is there a particular issue you need to clear up? Do you need to seek help with that communication?

Do you agree about "delayed gratification"? Are you both willing to be frugal now in the pursuit of wealth accumulation or do you agree to spend freely now to have what you want?

If you are about to make changes in your life it is essential to have good open communication between you about money and to recognize and respect each other's point of view.

Priorities

As we have said many times, the intention of this book is to enable you to create the life you want without financial compromise. It is useful in this process to prioritize your goals.

This is sometimes known as your "goal hierarchy". At the top of your hierarchy may be something financial, like buying a house or retiring or it may be something relating to the direction your life needs to take: the expression of a passion or new direction in your work. In cases where it really is not possible to pursue several goals at a time, look deeply within and prioritize. Whether you are single or in a relationship, establishing your priorities can help you move forward because things don't have to be let go of, maybe just delayed.

Here is a list of some of the more obvious things people name as priorities. Add your own to the list.

Which would you be prepared to put temporarily on the back burner? Which are you not prepared to delay? Look at your list and decide which ones rise to the top as essential for your soul *and* sense of security right now. If you are in a relationship, it may be important that both of you have your top priorities honored (if they are different) if you are to avoid resentment later. If they are different, make sure you design life so that at different times each of you has a time to focus on each person's priority.

This list assumes that the necessities for survival are covered.

Apart from the basics, how do you prioritize the list below, ignoring the ones you already have covered?

Home ownership/a different home

Saving for your own or your children's education

Vehicle ownership: car, RV, boat, plane, truck, bike, etc.

Travel and vacations

Eating out and entertainment

Savings for income during retirement/retiring.

Starting a project or business

Finding work that expresses who I am.

Finding my direction

Big adventures

Time to follow interests/play

Time to socialize

Time to relax

Feeling fulfilled by work

Finding joy in each of my days

Enjoying meaningful connections in my relationships

Time to be still and contemplative

I invite you to add your own...

Often people immediately recognize their priorities but to some, it may seem strange to have "a big adventure" in the same list as "home ownership" and "retirement savings". But we are talking about priorities here in the biggest sense to mean both "self-actualization" *and* material well-being. There is more to security than material well-being. What is important to you right now? What do you still need to feel complete? Remember it may change.

Are you aware of what your partner's priorities are? Share them with each other.

What are you doing financially to ensure that those priorities are being taken care of? Both yours and your partner's. What are you doing emotionally to ensure those priorities are addressed?

Home

Making changes may involve changing your living situation. How do you feel about that? Here are some questions to help you through a discussion about where you live:

How often are you prepared or excited to move if it becomes necessary?

Are you prepared to live in a "fixer"?

How important is "neighborhood" to you?

What kind of neighborhood do you prefer?

What kind/size of house do you prefer?

What size yard or piece of property do you want?

Is a sense of "community" important to you? What does that mean to you?

Do you want your house to be a project? In other words, how would you feel about selling your home every year to make money?

How do you feel about renting out part of your house?

How do you feel about renting the whole house if you are away?

If you have children, do you want to stay in the same house/school district throughout their schooling?

Do you want separate bedrooms for each child?

Do you prefer rural or urban living? If you want to live in a city, what size/which one?

Describe what your ideal living situation would be right now and in the future.

Travel

What part, if any, would you like travel to play in your life? One extreme may be if one or both of you wanted to travel constantly, for instance, as a teacher, journalist, filmmaker, doctor, engineer, etc. The other extreme would be being entirely based in one place taking a small trip occasionally. A third option may be to be based in one place but plan for "big adventures" either for work or not, throughout your lifetime.

Where are you on the spectrum? Where would you like to be? How do you see travel fitting into your life story, into your work story?

Retirement/Financial Independence

I like to differentiate between "Retirement" and "Financial Independence" because to me "Retirement" seems primarily to imply a cessation of working. "Financial Independence", on the other hand, seems to imply the possibility of productive, creative, and purposeful activities without them having to result necessarily in the production of money.

So, here are some questions to consider on this topic:

How much capital and/or income would allow you to feel Financially Independent?

Ideally, when would you like this to be your reality?

Do you both understand and agree about if/how you are planning for this?

If/when the work you do for money is also your calling, your fulfillment, your passion, and your dream, how long do you intend to continue doing it?

Describe to each other what you would like life to look like when you are financially independent.

If the work you do for money is not fulfilling your potential or your soul, would you rather:

...continue doing what you do but "Retire" sooner with less?

...pull out all stops, earn a lot more, and retire sooner with the desired amount?

...stick it out or,

...change what you do?

Almost undoubtedly, if you are a couple, there will be differences and divergences in your answers to these questions. But the more understanding there is of each other, the more each may be able to be flexible with his/her own priorities.

A healthy relationship allows for the enrichment and fulfillment of each partner and cannot be used as an excuse not to fully evolve as individuals. A healthy relationship allows for the growth of each individual *and* the partnership. Why use either your relationship or money as an excuse for not finding your own way?

Hopefully, these conversations with yourself and/or your partner(s) were illuminating, stimulating, and non-contentious. Hopefully, you now have a good understanding of all parties' needs and priorities as you take the next step through life.

Chapter 9 - *Making It Happen*

It's time to get specific, separate the plans into parts, prioritize, identify actions needed, and make a practical, financial plan, and a timeline. Soon you will be able to name the first step and take it!

But, before we start, there is one last question:

Do you have the mindset?

Without the mindset, nothing will happen.

Without the mindset, you will continue to use your relationship, your children, money, or something else, as an excuse not to act.

Is your intention strong enough to get you through the challenges?

Are you ready?

Re-open the doors to your longing and touch once again the thrill of creating your life, the thrill of waking with energy and excitement, of approaching each decision throughout your day as an opportunity, making each choice, conscious.

Look back to the work in chapter three where you connected to your Life Force and responded to the call of life. Remember your intuition about the life that would be the fullest expression of your best self.

In Chapter three you created the kernel of a dream.

Are you really ready to follow through?

This is the point at which you commit to living those ideas, not using money as an excuse but also *not* compromising the foundations of your security. Making it work on all levels.

If your heart and mind are open, life unfolds as it is meant to. A serendipitous suggestion or meeting, an unplanned activity or unexpected offer, and life takes off. At other times, the process takes more direction and management, at least initially, and this is the process we describe in this section.

Write your intention for change

Take time. Start by just moving through your days with new curiosity and heightened awareness that you are moving into a new way of being, into a new chapter.

When you are ready, using the notes you already have from Chapter 3, define and refine your desire, your intention, whatever it might be, large or small, that ignites the fire in your belly, and opens your soul.

This may require more research, and talking to more people. Get as specific as you can. When you are ready, write your plan. Keep it concise and precise, an elevator speech, a mission statement.

This could be anything from:

I will connect once a week to at least one person I love but am not in touch with.

I will try _____. I have always wanted to try _____ but have never found time.

I will tell my boss that I need _____ from my work.

I will learn to knit.

I will do _____ training so I can branch out.

I will start a business.

I will market my product/skill and build a clientele.

I will travel to _____, and do _____.

I will dive into other people's minds.

I will help children be the best they can be.

I will create _____ amount of time to reflect on my next chapter.

Of necessity, these are all vague, make yours specific.

Whatever it is, think about this intention during your days and, using your Witness, notice how you feel when your mind wanders in that direction. Do you feel a frisson of charge in your belly? Does a smile creep across your face? Does your mind return to your plan frequently?

Change your elevator speech as necessary until it feels right.

Speak your intention

When your written intention feels true, speak it. Speak it only to yourself. Is it your Truth?

When it feels true to yourself, speak it to those you are closest to, and people you feel totally safe with. Ask them to please just listen, not to give opinions or judgments.

Listen to your voice. When you are speaking your truth, it will sound powerful. Use the pronoun "I", even if you are in a relationship.

Adjust and refine more until you hear the power in your voice, until you know you are speaking your truth and the people you address, pay attention.

When you are ready, start saying it to others.

You will receive both negative and positive feedback. Notice how you feel when the feedback is negative. Does it make you question your choices? Do you still have the strength of your convictions?

Get organized

Divide your plan into its parts, from the very first step all the way to fruition. What needs to happen? What do you need to do? Brainstorm and write every tiny thing down.

What information do you need?

Where is that information?

What phone calls do you need to make?

Who do you need to meet with?

Who do you need to hire?

What equipment do you need?

Where do you acquire it?

Do you need training or education?

Where do you get it? How long does it take? What does it cost?

Where do you find the financial information/help you need?

From these questions (and more) create a comprehensive to-do list.

Put the list into logical chronological order.

Make a feasible timeline for each step, with specific dates by which each task will be both initiated and completed.

Give yourself the time you need because it is important to stick to the timeline. Put the start date, each deadline, and completion date on your calendar in big red letters. Your timeline may spread over days, weeks, or years. Stick to it.

Pause

This step is so important and must be given adequate time. You decide how much time.

Up until now the process has been proactive, ordered, directed, and driven. Now we allow for some space. The seeds are planted, some plans are made but nothing is cast in stone, and no money spent. You have not yet pulled the trigger.

Now is the time to get out of the way and allow life to happen. With the seeds sown you will move through life differently even if you are not doing anything to make those seeds germinate. But your attention will be drawn differently. You will notice differently; you will take in different stimuli and information. The seeds may germinate of their own accord, they may wither, they may just settle in and subliminally become your new norm.

It is important during this period not to try to achieve anything. Just watch. Leave the control seat and get out of your own way. Watch what happens with curiosity.

It is possible that you may feel an increasing sense of urgency and literally not be able to wait a moment longer before you take the first step. Great!

On the other hand, you may feel an increasing sense that in fact you planted the wrong variety of seed. Great! Start over.

Stay honest and flexible throughout the whole period. One thing leads to another. Sometimes we find the road we are heading down is simply not our road. But, in the meantime, other avenues may have opened. Be prepared for U-turns. Be prepared to admit failure, quit, and start over on a new track. You may never find the new track without having started on the original one. See "failure" not as a negative but as one of the most potent teachers. Transformation grows from experimentation, failure and figuring out new ways.

The important thing is that your approach to life has changed. Now, as you consider each decision you make during a day you consider it with the filter of how it enlivens or deadens you, whether it is routine and habitual or whether it is creative and inspiring.

Try to get used to the idea of change being natural, frequent, and on-going, not something to avoid. Embrace change as it beckons.

Maybe at the end of your pause things will look entirely different and you may need to go through the first 4 steps again.

Make a Financial Plan

The possibilities for change are of course as endless as the people on this planet and each change has its own specific prerequisites and costs. The following list illustrates the point that some dreams are free, some require a small infusion of cash, and some require an extensive business plan along with detailed financial strategies.

Travel in India and live in an ashram.

Invent a product and start a company.

Sail the world and write about it

Teach in an African orphanage

Create a unique line of clothing

Coach a kids' soccer team

Become a gourmet cook

Dance the Tango

Make a movie

Become an electrician

Write a poem

Mentor a child

Restore a vintage car

Build an ecolodge

Make a new friend

Learn a language

Learn to be still

There will be preparation and costs for whatever is waiting to come into your life. When you have your chronological to-do list, do the research, and add the costs, if any, to each item.

Consider how your plan will impact your current financial situation. If it involves a considerable change to your current income, make a detailed financial plan of how you will meet your obligations during the change. If it involves borrowing from existing savings, plan to repay that amount.

When you have a good understanding of the altered financial reality you are facing, return to Chapter 6 and identify the strategies that can facilitate your goals. Make sure, as always, that you watch your emotional reactions at this stage and be sure to recognize when fear, anxiety or stress arise. These strategies must be *yours*. They must be strategies that you can live with, enjoy, through the upcoming period of change.

The goals may change, and if they do, the financial plan will shift too. But start with a framework and adjust it as necessary, as things evolve.

The case studies in Chapter 10 exemplify how people have used many of these tools.

I am not suggesting that any one of them is appropriate for you as your solution. They are intended to stimulate your own research and to inspire a desire to think creatively about making things work.

Each situation is entirely different, and you cannot make a successful decision without considering your age, your assets, your priorities, and the specifics of your and your family's needs. If you are considering making a big change in your financial life, you should consult a Financial Planner by the hour to help you. Not only will they be able to explain the specific implications of any change you make to your situation, but they will also be able to explain how the specific details of any financial system you are contemplating, work. For instance, if your plan requires raising considerable sums of money, you may consider re-prioritizing your long-term savings plan for a period. The Financial Planner would help with that.

Start with the first item on the to-do list

Consult your timeline...***DO IT!***

Here is an example of a project timeline. This was created by a young couple who had good office jobs in the city. Their dream was to make a documentary film of the ancient stories told by aboriginal peoples of Australia. They wanted to take a sabbatical year from their jobs to gather their material in Australia then return to their jobs and create the film in their spare time. They intended to leave for Australia in 2 years.

If the film project was successful, they would eventually embark on a second film project. The couple had studied film and photography at university and had accumulated a fair amount of equipment along the way. They wanted to have children after the first film was complete and hoped to take the children along as they traveled, collecting data for the second project. They wanted to buy a house before they left in 2 years, so they didn't get priced out of the housing market and had a home base. They intended to rent it out to cover the mortgage while they were away. They wanted to start retirement savings and intended to start college savings for children as soon as they were born.

Within the next 2 years

Purchase house/apartment. Price **$250,000**

20% down = **$50,000**

(They already have $40,000 saved between them)

$10,000 needed

Purchase air tickets to Australia

$3,000 needed

Purchase photographic equipment
$1,000 needed

Purchase secondhand Jeep in Australia
$5,000 needed

Save funds to live for 1 year in Australia

$25,000 needed

 $44,000 = **Total needed.**

Solutions:

- Immediately research lending institutions to establish the best lending option for their house purchase.
- Immediately research property for sale in the neighborhood and start making offers.
- If possible, purchase a home asap and rent out a room. Save all rent proceeds.
- Write an info sheet about the project. Distribute to all family and friends and ask for all gifts (Xmas and birthdays) in cash over the next 2 years. Save every penny in a separate account.
- Initiate a Kickstarter (fundraising) campaign.
- Establish domestic austerity and cut expenses as much as possible. Make sure all savings are regularly deposited in a separate Project account.
- Network with filmmakers regarding funding/grants/acquisition of equipment.
- Talk to the bank about a home equity line of credit on the house after the house purchase.
- Consider overtime at work and save every penny.
- Talk to publishers and film distributors about an "advance" on the project. Even if it doesn't bear fruit they will get the word out, make contacts and familiarize themselves with talking about the project.
- Write directly to foundations for grants.
- Talk on the local radio, at the local library, etc. to spread enthusiasm, information and possibly raise funds.

Each of these tasks had a specific timeline noted on their schedule.

During this two-year period, they were able to make a detailed to-do list and timeline for the next phase. They spent time researching their project, planning their route, and working on the structure of their film.

Have fun making your plans happen.

If your heart is singing, follow it...

Chapter 10 - *Case Studies*

These are case studies of people who have kept life juicy. Some are still doing what they first set out to do. Others have continued to make changes. None are bored.

Creating the life you want is truly an art form; the art of constructing your unique tapestry, sometimes one thread at a time, sometimes with sweeping swathes of color. Sometimes with subtle suggestions of shading.

It is choosing to focus on what feeds you, and moving in that direction.

It is the art of meeting each transition with an open mind and eager curiosity, of prioritizing the sweet gift of vitality. It is constantly remembering the brevity of life and rather than letting it slip on by, or shuffling through it, expanding horizons, and greeting opportunities with courage and flexibility.

I hope that you have dived deep into the core of your being, touching, and feeling your uniqueness.

I also hope that you have a realistic understanding of your relationship with money, of your financial situation, and the ways money can assist you on your journey.

I hope you have taken a long look at your need for "security" and ways of nurturing it. And that you have arrived with some nascent dreams that rekindle your spark and nourish your soul.

The main work is done. You are ready to take one comfortable, easy step at a time, guided by your animating force within. Continue to watch yourself with discernment and honesty, and life will become a fascinating open book.

Either you will initiate your next steps yourself, or opportunities will come knocking on your door, inviting you to respond instinctively. Or you may find your joy in simply being, the way things are.

The stories illustrate many solutions people found to express their fullest self, without compromising, often greatly improving, their financial situation. I hope the ideas inspire and help you to recognize your own unique solutions.

All names of the storytellers have been changed to protect privacy.

Peter's Story

Just one or two clients can provide you freedom.

Peter was aware at a young age that he was not going to fit the mold that others chose for him. This came to a head when he graduated from university and found himself turning down numerous good job offers that would have started him on the first rung of that ladder.

No matter how lucrative the career opportunity, his heart screamed "No".

Then serendipity tapped him on the shoulder and finally, he found himself uttering a resounding: "Yes" to something that truly excited him.

As you will see, once he had taken the initial step, he was able to craft his life by using his skills creatively. I asked Peter if he had navigated transitions by making big decisions and changes or whether the process had just evolved. He replied that he had literally "jumped off the cliff without wings" 2 or 3 times in his life but that daily, constantly, he continues to make little decisions to readjust the course.

Peter had been raised and educated in a way that would lead automatically to a well-paying, professional career with a predictable path to the top. But even from his early teens, Peter had known that the idea of anything "predictable" was not what he wanted. He did not want to sell his soul to the company store and climb the corporate ladder.

So, unbeknown to his parents, when he was offered several "promising" positions, he turned them all down! At each interview, he looked across the desk at the middle-aged interviewer and knew he was looking at himself 30 years hence and saw the intervening years simply evaporate before his eyes.

Even as a young man, he knew instinctively he was not prepared to forfeit his life for a secure, but uninspired path toward retirement. The job he would eventually accept was as a journalist, partly because it promised the opportunity for adventure, but also because it provided significant freedom. He started the job but always with an eye on the horizon for more.

One day in his early twenties he was invited onto a sailing yacht for a social event and this gathering changed his life. By the time he stepped ashore after the party, he had been offered a job. This time, not knowing what he was signing up for, never having set foot on a sailboat before, he accepted wholeheartedly!

This was the first cliff Peter jumped off with no guarantees of the outcome.

It turned out he had agreed to help crew the boat across the Pacific Ocean. The job had no future, very little money, no security, but Peter felt alive, excited and energized. As he now muses: "Saying *yes* to that invitation led to a world of possibilities I could never have imagined." And the idea of "unknown possibilities" was very attractive, the draw of the unknown was powerful to him. He requested and was granted, a year's leave of absence from the journalism job.

During the 6,000-mile ocean voyage, Peter came to realize that he was a sailor, that sailing was what brought him joy, and that "a life on the ocean waves" indeed, was the only life for him.

Peter learned on that voyage that he wanted sailing to be a big part of his life. He had also figured out that he wanted his own boat, and he wanted his Captain's license. On the other hand, he had also come to realize that he wanted a steady and healthy income source to fund this adventurous life in style and comfort. He had none of the above. But he had his dream. He knew his purpose.

Peter started his research and found that one way to own a yacht was through a Charter Company. He found the perfect boat and placed it in charter for several years during which time Peter could only use it for several weeks a year. He spent this time studying for and getting his Captain's License and returned to his job as a journalist to pay down the loan on the boat as quickly as possible. Before he knew it, he had his boat, his Captain's license and was free to go sailing, submitting stories of his high sea's adventures to his editor! The plan was falling into place. Then Peter met the love of his life. He had no intention of settling down and marrying, he was a confirmed salty bachelor.

Once more he felt the pull towards the cliff and once again, he jumped! Peter and Marie were married.

He now had a wonderful wife and a ready-made 2-year-old, and they headed to the Caribbean on their sailboat. Together they took out charter groups and

Peter continued to write and sell his stories. Peter's wife, Marie, is a highly experienced massage therapist and her skills were greatly appreciated by many people and guests they met on their voyages.

And here you might imagine this idyllic story ends. But as we know, the only constant is change and after several years, even floating around the Caribbean needed some adjustment. Peter found himself bored easily with doing just one thing. The couple still wanted to be cruising but they wanted variety, especially of income. They did not want to be tied to chartering anymore and that was a problem as chartering was their main source of income, so they started to consider options. Peter looked at his skills: he was a ship's captain and a writer of stories! Marie was a masseuse.

Together they networked contacts and soon Peter was in touch with a man who owned a big, wonderful boat on the lake near their hometown. The owner of the boat entertains on his boat during the summer months and now employs Peter to skipper his boat.

Simultaneously Peter was also able to use his writing skills as the perfect tool to start a Public Relations company. During their months at sea Peter and Marie had, of necessity, become very adept at using social media. Peter was able to fill a niche for successful businesspeople who had neither the skills nor the time to represent themselves in this way. Peter has now built a very profitable business, sitting on his foredeck, creating wonderful images for his clients, and broadcasting them worldwide!

Peter and Marie now spend the summer months at home, skippering a beautiful boat on a gorgeous lake, and the "winter" months choosing their cruising grounds and sailing away!

Marie owns a spa and helps her clients in the summer months at home with therapeutic massage. She continues to practice her skills as they sail in the winter to help people they meet on the way.

This life stimulates and challenges them and fills their souls with the natural beauty of our planet. They have 3 grandchildren and when I asked Peter how they manage to see them with this full life he replied: "It is not our job to parent them, we don't need to be with them all the time. We want to create peak experiences for them that they will never forget. We want to change their lives when we are with them. We want to make real things happen. Life is banal.... let's create the special moments"

Observations

- Prioritize self-knowledge and stay true to yourself as you make each decision.
- Say "Yes" when opportunity knocks if it feels right, on a visceral level. Respond from the gut. If the "yes" is strong enough, go with it!
- Maintain clarity and conviction, be honest and do not compromise on your priorities. "Design the dream, make the plan, and PUT THE DATE ON THE CALENDAR. Then build the life one piece at a time, adjusting as necessary."
- Find one or two clients who pay you well: this can buy you freedom. One of the big keys to Peter's

freedom was finding just a few clients who paid him enough for his PR skills. This provided the financial freedom to pursue other adventures.
- Learn new skills and hone the ones you already have. Peter honed his ability to tell stories into a successful Public Relations business and broadened his range by mastering the niceties of social media.

Peter and Marie chose to create a life of adventure, beauty, and creativity on the road less travelled. They chose not to follow someone else's path. They chose not to follow a predetermined path. They chose to create a life that energizes and inspires them, that is not "normal". They are creating experiences that feed their souls. They feel alive and certainly do not watch the clock or look forward to Friday night!

Their life is not for everyone, but their creativity may help to inspire *your* dreams.

Nora's Story

Be prepared to move outside your comfort zone and learn to love that.

The next story starts out on Sunday evenings.

Nora and her family enjoyed a particular TV show on Sunday evenings that came to signify the end of the weekend and a time to psychologically adjust to the upcoming week. This had always been a time to switch gears and look forward to the week ahead with keen anticipation.

Then something changed. Over time Nora became aware of:

"A gnawing, sinking feeling in the pit of my belly as I stared down at the week ahead, not with glee and anticipation, but with a definite flatness".

Nora was a successful and much-loved teacher but for whatever reason, the joy had run out and she was "flatlining" as we described in earlier chapters. It was time to either make a change or wither on the vine.

Unlike Peter in our previous story, Nora did not initially make big decisions or changes. She did not start out by jumping off the cliff. She did not design the dream, plan, and put a start date on the calendar.

Nora's process was more gradual. First, she noticed the Sunday night syndrome. The next sign that something was about to shift happened while she and her family were traveling. They had always prioritized travel and organized extraordinary adventures to exotic faraway places.

It was on one such trip that Nora started to notice that her eyes were constantly on the look-out for ideas, for products that could inspire the genesis of a business and a possible exit strategy from teaching. Everywhere she went she went with eyes wide open, seeing things in a new light, open to inspiration. Eventually something landed and took hold.

As Nora's need for change became more and more of a reality for her, the desire to develop her own product and start her own business, began to grow.

As her dreams took shape, she began to feel alive, energized, motivated, excited. She knew there would be risk, long hours, and the possibility of failure but she couldn't wait to pour herself into her business.

"It was terrifying but quite clear. The other option deadened me".

Nora set to work designing and refining her product and eventually was happy with the result. It met all her specifications: it was practical, sustainable, beautiful, lightweight, useful and in line with Nora's values. She was eager and proud to offer this product to the world. With the blessings of her family, she took the plunge. But, unlike Peter who describes his plunge as "off a cliff without wings" Nora describes her plunge as:

"Small steps, I knew my limits and I knew I had to keep stress under control".

The main fear for Nora and her husband was financial. As teachers they had a comfortable life, were able to travel and were confident they could cope with college expenses for their daughter in a few years' time. If they gave up their jobs before they knew the business was viable, they would have been giving up a lot: salary, full benefits, paid vacation, growth of Retirement savings etc...in other words everything that represented security for them.

Eventually, the upside outweighed the risk and Nora was ready. Otherwise, she would have had to give up feeling alive. She took small steps at first.

As Nora developed her product, she kept her teaching position and eventually got the business up and running entirely from her home. They resisted borrowing money for premises or employees for as long as possible. The business was launched by borrowing money from their Retirement accounts, from their emergency fund, savings, and with small loans from their parents. They cut back living expenses in any way they could and managed to scrape together enough to produce sufficient product to get started. Before long, their house was stacked from floor to ceiling with boxes, papers, and equipment!

The first year was hugely stressful, despite only taking small steps. But they chose their stress. They could handle long hours and hard work, but they couldn't handle the idea of debt...yet.

The challenges came thick and fast even without the challenge of debt. Nora felt the full weight of responsibility on her shoulders.

"I was risking the family savings; the quality of our daily lives was unrecognizable, and I was stressed to my limit," she says, "and for a whole year we got no results for all our efforts."

Nora describes two of the major hurdles she had to overcome during this year. The first was the naysayers, the skeptics, the dis-approvers. Whether from love and concern or even a little jealousy other people react when we make dramatic changes to our lives and sometimes the reactions can be less than supportive. Nora remembers being constantly informed by concerned folk:

"Nine out of ten businesses fail you know."

It took a lot of strength not to be influenced by the skeptics when she herself felt the most doubtful of all. Nothing initially was leading her to believe that success was just around the corner. As she says of that time:

"I just kept going. And kept going".

The other challenge for Nora was having to step firmly out of her comfort zone.

"I found it excruciating to make cold calls with the intention of selling my own product." she recalls.

But she persevered, trying one avenue after another to advertise her product through the channels that would reach the buyers she needed.

Eventually, their luck turned with two simultaneous events. The first was the airing of a TV show demonstrating the need for products like hers. The second was an article in Sunset magazine singing their praises. The coincidence of these two events led directly to the market they needed. They had found their audience; they could now advertise directly to their audience and things started to flow.

The phone started ringing off the hook and they saw the green light. They ran with it and organized so they could handle the increase in volume. The product was being manufactured overseas so they could increase the scale of production.

At the start of the second year, Nora dropped to half-time teaching for the year, but after that, her contract was not renewable. But by that time, she did feel comfortable enough to jump off the cliff and she gave up her job. They were officially "in business" and over the ensuing years enjoyed both the rewards and challenges this new life brought.

In order to grow the business, they did borrow money, and each time they did it was challenging, each time was a leap off a cliff for them. They have no regrets and have now moved on, yet again to the next adventures life will bring.

This inspiring story shows how two people with very few assets, and no experience, started a business and grew it to considerable success. They worked incredibly hard, they evolved and changed and grew with the business and never regretted taking the risks they took. Never again did they feel that sinking feeling as they faced down a new week.

Observations
- Take small steps. Choose what kind of stress you can handle, know your limits, and keep it under control.

- Work hard if the work feeds you.
- Don't be sabotaged by skeptics and critics.
- Be prepared to move outside your comfort zone and learn to love doing it. Fake it to make it.
- Stay flexible and open to new ideas. Stay ahead of the curve. When you bump into a new idea that wasn't part of your original plan, if it's good, adjust and go with it.
- Be prepared for domestic (and professional) austerity. In order to survive the hard times, learn to do with less and use it as an opportunity for creativity.
- Be prepared to borrow when you feel the green light. Develop a good and lasting relationship with a lender or bank that you trust and take them with you every step of the way.
- And the biggest advice in Nora's opinion: Let go. Do not try to control, or do everything. Other people have realms of expertise you don't have. Let them help you make decisions. Often a business owner is too close to the details to see the bigger picture. Let someone else envision your big picture and allow the outcome even if it wasn't your original idea.

David's Story

Work overseas, save and be patient.

David's story illustrates how life can turn on a dime. In his case, he had to hit rock bottom before being able to seek a way up and out.

For David, several events converged simultaneously to precipitate the bottom. His marriage failed and ended in divorce. He was working at a job with no future and low remuneration. Since the divorce, he was the sole owner of a house he had recently bought with his ex-wife and was carrying a large mortgage alone.

He knew: "This isn't enough". He was 29 and hit a very low spot. The bottom had fallen out of his life.

Serendipitously, in the nick of time, David bumped into an old friend who was in a similar situation and as they shared their stories over a beer one night, the friend announced that he had taken a job in Saudi Arabia, teaching English as a Foreign Language.

Although he had no previous experience in this field, David was intrigued and started to research similar opportunities. He found he could earn an extremely good income, tax-free in UK pounds, with all expenses paid! He applied for a job and very quickly secured a position.

At this point, David was not so much moving toward something that really attracted him, as moving away from a bad situation. He said it felt like jumping off a cliff without a parachute, like diving into "the war zone" but he was so ready to find a way to make changes in his life that he forged ahead anyway. He was open to whatever showed up in this new life and confident that when the financial problems were alleviated, he would be able to envision a future that he desired.

David spent five years in Saudi Arabia, had an amazing social life, traveled all over the world, met fascinating people, and at the end of the five years had saved enough money to buy (for cash) a beautiful apartment in a very desirable part of England.

He was also able to devise a plan for his future that really excited him. Without the pressures, he was feeling before he left home, with more time available, and with the stimulation of new people, places, and activities, he became surer of his identity and the direction that was truly authentic for him.

His plan was to enroll in university and study for his master's degree in Education and then teach English to foreign students who were entering the English university system.

Meanwhile, he had met and married his new wife, and the money he had made abroad supported them while he attended University for two years for his graduate degree.

After graduation, they rented out their home and traveled abroad again for a while. Eventually, David found his dream position in a prestigious university in the town where they lived. David was teaching international students in a Graduate School and enjoyed a successful career that stimulated him till the day he retired.

Observations

- David's story illustrates the idea of creating different chapters in life. He was in a serious financial (and emotional) bind and because of that, he was not able to take the next step towards his goal: becoming a university teacher. He sorted his finances first and waited to implement his long-term goals.
- David's story teaches the necessity of keeping your eye on the ball. He continued to make changes and did not get stuck. Unlike other people he worked with in Saudi Arabia, he knew when he had made enough money. He did not become addicted to money for its own sake. He kept his goal in mind and returned home to get the qualifications he needed.
- Yet again, David's story shows the necessity of sometimes just taking a risk. He had nothing to lose so opted for the unknown in order to achieve a goal later, but the unknown turned out to be full of unexpected and delightful opportunities.

Sally's Story

Pay attention to Attention.

Sally's story teaches how transformation can at once be subtle and dramatic. Unlike our previous stories, Sally did not change her country, her home, or even her career, but the changes she did make transformed her life.

Perhaps the most significant lesson her story illustrates is the power of Attention.

Sally is a nurse practitioner and at the time that our story begins, she held a very prestigious and secure position as Director of the Medical Center at the local university. After many years in this position, Sally noticed that her attention was becoming more and more focused on one very specific aspect of her work: women's sexuality. As she told me:

"I literally felt myself coming alive when presented with issues involving women's sexuality. I felt more and more of my being was engaged, that a bigger part of me responded to each situation. This awareness came directly from my core, from my center, beyond mere intellectual interest. The entire complexity of my personality, the part of me that is teacher, healer, goddess, mother, friend, all of me was alert, alive, engaged, all parts of me engaged, my whole self."

Sally's attention was her guide. It seemed during these months that it had a life of its own, it led her directly and repeatedly to women's sexual issues.

Eventually, she experienced an "Ah ha" moment after which there was no turning back. Sally knew she had to honor her passion, and make a shift in her work, so she could focus entirely on female sexuality.

The moment came after Sally had administered a routine pap test and was asking the patient all the important and probing questions. Sally was overwhelmed by the absolute preciousness of the human being in her care.

In that moment of interaction Sally's insight about who she was and how she was driven to lead her life, was conscious. The conscious and unconscious were, at that moment, aligned and she indeed experienced a "moment of knowing", a moment of knowing deeply who she is.

Sally is lucky. She is highly attuned to where her Attention leads her and is able to follow its guide until she knows what is true for her.

Around this time, Sally was a speaker at a university health conference in Las Vegas. While there, she heard a psychologist lecture and was fascinated. Her attention was riveted. She realized he was standing where she wanted to be standing, immersed in the topic of "people as they intersected with their sexuality." She started to explore where she could learn more about the field of sexual medicine and began studying with sexual experts from Boston to Los Angeles.

Sally started to consider the possibility of re-directing her career and as she did, she felt an uninhibited:" Yes". She embraced her decision wholeheartedly. Things started to fall into place, but not without risk.

Sally was a single mother with two small children, a mortgage, and significant responsibilities. So, for a while, she did nothing, until she started experiencing headaches and could no longer ignore the call of change.

The idea of moving from being employed, with benefits, to self-employed with none, was certainly a risky proposition. But Sally had numerous contacts in the medical world and as she interacted with them, they encouraged her decision to make a change.

Soon she was approached by a colleague and owner of a medical practice who invited Sally to join her practice. Sally would start part-time and build her clientele. This was not ideal as Sally really needed to work full-time, but she grabbed the opportunity and was patient.

We can remember Goethe's saying here: "For those who make a move, the Universe will follow". Things started falling into place.

That very night Sally saw an advertisement in the paper for a part-time position at the university where she currently worked. She applied and was accepted. She resigned as Director of the Medical Center and was filled with relief. She had taken several big steps towards her dream while taking care of herself and her sons. She had shifted the picture, taken important steps, cut the tie of her very demanding job, and moved towards her goal, with patience. She was now working part-time in a self-employed capacity and made up for the loss in salary with the part-time position at the university.

When her own practice was built to 4 days a week she quit the job at the university, relinquished her Emeritus faculty status, and took a significant reduction in income. By this time, she felt confident enough with her new direction, to take the increased risk.

For a while Sally tightened her belt, and was content with less, trusting that this was temporary. She budgeted, improvised, and worked hard until her practice was all she wanted it to be, and she was back on track financially. During this time, she repeated her Mantra: "Money, please be my friend, don't leave me now, I've been good to you." I'm not sure about the science of Mantras but I do know that in moments of anxiety it certainly helps to repeat and believe something positive and kind.

Her work has blossomed and expanded. Sally now gives lectures and workshops in her field of expertise, has written a book, and intends to be able to reach out and help thousands of women worldwide to reach their potential as fulfilled sexual human beings.

Observations

- Learn to pay attention to your Attention.

- Have the courage to explore all avenues even if many lead nowhere.
  - Take the first step. It is certain nothing will happen if you don't.
  - Be patient. Build the dream step by step.
  - Pay attention to your body and the messages it is sending you.
  - Trust that times of austerity will be temporary.
  - Monitor progress until you reach the tipping point then go for it.
  - Befriend Money.

Susan's Story

Don't get paralyzed by following your bliss, but never give up on Bliss.

Susan grew up poor, one of five children, with a single Mom. Consequently, she is no dreamer when it comes to money. Susan knows all too well that without a paycheck, bills will not get paid, and food will not arrive on the table.

But even though money is important to her, she has never sold her soul to the paycheck. She has never stagnated in a position if it meant literally withering inside, if it meant her Life-force was shriveling. And Susan has not merely stayed alive, she has blossomed, she has followed her muse *and* made a good living.

Because of the austerity of her childhood, she has never been prepared to jeopardize financial security *and* she has never felt the need to forfeit what she describes as her "Ju Ju", her creative spirit, and her passions. She has learned that her passions can be fulfilled from many sources, simultaneously.

For reasons that will become clear, she has been able to stay employed to maintain financial security *and* she has been able to live a wildly creative, adventurous, and spiritual life.

Fresh from High School, Susan's priority was to secure a job and earn money. At first, she wasn't as concerned about fulfillment from a job as a flow of income to cover living expenses.

But over the years she has found ways to express the many diverse sides of herself wherever she finds herself, be it work or play. In fact, the line between "work" and "play" has softened; for Susan, both are opportunities to expand fully into who she is. She has created integration between her many roles in life, and interconnectivity both inside and outside her job.

Initially, Susan's life started out somewhat compartmentalized. Her job provided money, but everything else happened after hours.

This worked for several years. Until it didn't. She needed to find ways to express more of herself during working hours.

She describes this as having a "slash career". At the time of our interview, she described herself as an executive, a coach, a spiritual counselor, a teacher, and a poet. But when asked about what she *does*, she responded with the bigger picture: "I am the creative fire that ignites in others their own love poem from God." And this she does, wherever she finds herself in each moment: boardroom /classroom /hospital/Mexican Retreat. She finds ways to support what people want and to support them as they dream for themselves.

This is how Susan's story unfolds:

Her first job was a position with a Telephone company. Simultaneously she enrolled in college to finish her undergraduate degree and even managed to save money so she could build a house.

Over the years, Susan found ways to make this seemingly dull job more fulfilling. She also found ways to follow her passion outside her corporate work: building a house, finishing her doctorate, producing an album of music, publishing books of poetry, teaching at the local college, and even building a Villa in Mexico. The Telephone company paid full tuition for her master's degree and later, gave her 3 months off to complete her doctoral dissertation. Her corporate job was an asset in more ways than one.

Susan loved the people she worked with, and the daily requirements were interesting enough. When opportunities presented inside her job, she jumped at them. She was able to explore interests that she had not imagined would be possible within the corporate setting. She became a "diversity trainer" for the company and traveled to fourteen states to improve the cultural image of the company.

Her job at the telephone company even supported her when she was drawn to teach at a university. They gave her an Education "sabbatical" leave of absence and assurance that she would have a job when she returned.

Susan had been able to use the corporate system to fulfill many of her lifelong ambitions and develop new skills. *And* it provided the financial security she wanted.

Even though Susan had expanded the parameters of her job to express more of herself, there did come a time when she realized that, despite the variety and satisfaction she had, the more creative parts of her were calling for more. And the noise of that voice was getting louder.

Eventually, she left her long-time position before Retirement and began to teach full-time at the University and as always, one thing led to another. She was offered a teaching job in Greece. Both these teaching experiences were wonderful and exciting. They fed Susan's love of helping develop the souls and passions of her students. But after a few years on a professor's stipend, the money was running out! She gladly returned, once again, to her long-term job with the Directory Company for a few more years.

Susan realized that for her, being too anxious about finances lessened her creativity. But she was certainly not prepared to abandon the joy she had found in teaching.

"If I can't get *enough* Ju Ju on the inside of the job, I need to create more on the outside."

So now her financial needs were again being met on the inside, and Susan creates her "slash career" where she expresses the diverse sides of her being in different roles. She became a spiritual counselor at the local hospital, continues her executive teaching one evening a week, and travels to her Villa in Mexico to relax and write.

She now feels a sense of wholeness, not by throwing the baby out with the bathwater and *only* "following her Bliss", but rather by doing it all and finding her Bliss in every role.

The last time I spoke to Susan she was preparing to lead a tour in Bali, working on her third book of poetry, and overseeing the management of her Villa in Mexico. A different combination in her "slash career", but in a way, doing the same thing she has always done: taking care of her passions *and* financial responsibility.

Observations:

- If you are in a position that primarily meets financial needs, get creative in that situation, and use every opportunity to make it fulfill every side of you.
- If you still can't find enough fulfillment from within your job, create it on the outside.
- Recognize the integration between all your roles by expressing your true self in them all. Find the bliss in each role, in each moment.
- Create the security you need to free up time/money for your passion and never let go of the passion.
- Finding Bliss is subtle, not a big drama. In the big picture, it doesn't necessarily happen all in one place. Do what's "pleasant" and necessary, and make subtle moves towards what's next.
- Don't get paralyzed by "Following your Bliss". Don't let Finding your Bliss get in the way of the Bliss that's already there, all around you!

My Own Story

Continuity and change.

I have had 7 careers: teaching, motherhood, sea captain, business owner, financial planner, builder, and yoga instructor. I have had 2 husbands and two sons. I have enjoyed living in 3 different countries and enjoyed them all.

I have never felt I had just one single burning passion in life. But my capacity for passion is considerable and I enjoyed every path I trod. Until I didn't. Then I learned the importance of making change when it calls.

Here are some of the lessons that, had I known them at the time, would have helped most as I navigated the tides of change.

I will call the first lesson "moments of knowing", the sort of knowing that is felt in the body, viscerally, a "gut feeling". Along with most of our storytellers, I take those moments very seriously and have never forgotten them. These are moments of undeniable clarity. I have had several and each one has led to significant change.

One occurred while I was teaching at a university in Canada. I was summoned to the Dean's office.

She proceeded to offer me a primo job, full tenure with a full pension, the best medical, optical, and dental benefits, and paid vacation.

Security on a plate!

But as she was speaking, I began to feel an overwhelming sensation of a noose tightening around my neck. My stomach was tight, and it felt as if a dark curtain was being lowered over my whole being. The lights were going out.

She finished her speech and awaited my jubilation.

"And what do you want in return?" I asked. "My life?" It was clear that she had not described the life I craved.

Moments of knowing are powered by our intuition, delivered with such a powerful punch that they surely hold the gem of our Truth. When I have paid attention to them, I feel a strong sense of Self.

The second invaluable lesson is that of compartmentalization. Life can have many different phases of all different colors and flavors. I needed those different phases and longed to embrace each one as it arrived. I craved unpredictability and creativity! I longed for a life of change that could allow the expression of each part of my complex self.

Typically, Financial Planners advise that we pay attention to finances first, and stack up however many millions we are supposed to need to retire.

I did it the other way round and it worked, at least for me.

In my late twenties, I was cruising happily around the Mediterranean with the man of my dreams. One evening, anchored in a delightful cove, we met a retired couple, also sailing on their yacht, who leaned into us and advised sagely: "What are you two doing? These are your best earning years. You should be back home making a living so you can afford to go sailing when you retire".

This moment was powerful for me as they had named my greatest fear: I would live forever in poverty as a result of foolish irresponsible behavior in my youth! But on a deeper level, I knew that we were spending a few years of our precious youth in the most expansive, exciting way and I knew this was right for us. I didn't want to wait till I was old before my adventures began.

It turned out there was plenty of time to earn money, both before, after, and even during the adventure. The adventure stands out as one of the most significant periods of my life that I would not have missed for anything.

If I had known there would be time for it all, I could have relaxed into each phase more completely and watched each one unfold just as it was meant to.

The third lesson is to know when each chapter is complete and to have the courage to change. To let go when the juice has run dry.

Idyllic though the sailing was, eventually I felt the need to be in one place, to explore new avenues, be of service to others and be entrepreneurial.

So, when opportunity literally came knocking at my door, I welcomed it with a loud: "yes" and jumped into a totally new realm of expertise for me. I studied enthusiastically and enjoyed many years of owning a Financial Planning practice with 3 female partners.

We built a successful and growing company where we felt both productive and effective. I could not have done that twenty years previously. If anyone had suggested that I would one day become a Financial Planner I would have laughed at the absurdity. But things changed and when the time was right, I embraced it wholeheartedly.

There was so much about this profession that I loved. I was so grateful for my wonderful clients and the opportunity they gave me to share their lives. I loved working with my partners, designing, growing, and changing our business. As a younger person, I had no idea that any of these skills or interests were a part of who I am, and I am grateful that I was open to letting them emerge.

So, I had a lot to let go of when I realized my Light had gone out and this chapter too was at an end. There were other sides of me that were calling for attention.

Eventually, I was able to make the break. I studied once again and became a yoga instructor!

Change, for me, is challenging and exhilarating. Whatever ends, be it a big adventure, a previously fulfilling job, a home, a relationship, a good salary, even a stressful job, I have been both terrified and very excited. And making change has kept me alive and in love with life.

Initially, when I know I am in a period of transition I feel mainly fear and resistance. The thought of the unknown, upheaval, of speaking out, of upsetting my own and other people's equilibrium, is exhausting and frightening. All this initially seems insurmountable. Then the light starts to filter back in, and I can embrace what is coming next.

An ongoing lesson is to understand the power that money is capable of exerting over me.

The hardest changes to make are when they involve walking away from a healthy, predictable salary. I have done this many times and never regretted it. When the salary came at the cost of my spark, it was no longer worth it. When I started to spend my days watching the clock, then I knew it was time to look at what was holding me to the job.

And as I looked more deeply at my resistance to change, I was gradually able to name my demon: Money. My deep-rooted need for financial security was tweaked every time I considered change and particularly if I considered leaving a well-paying position.

Gradually I peeled away the layers of my relationship with money, I started to understand how and why it had such a hold on me. A hold that literally dictated the direction of my life.

I learned that the fear was not of being poor in the sense of not having enough to eat or clothes to wear. I knew I could always do something to earn money to feed and clothe myself and my family. It was the *shame* of not appearing successful to the world. Of not being good enough. Of losing respect. That was my fear, the possibility of appearing "less than" to others.

"Money has become a playing field where we measure our competence and worth as people".

The Soul of Money *by* Lynne Twist

Once I illuminated that (and much more), it dissipated, and it released its grip.

I then understood that I would honor my need for financial security but instead of allowing it to keep me stuck, I would find creative solutions to meet my needs.

I now look forward to the rest of my life unfolding and full of adventures!

Observations:

- Pay attention to "gut feelings" ...moments of knowing your Truth.
- If you have many disparate loves in life, remember that you can have time for them all.
- Recognize when each chapter has run its course and have the courage to change.
- Take a good look at your relationship with money.

My hope is that the pages of this book will have inspired you to find your Truth, the integrity to honor it, and the courage to make change, when and if it calls.

My hope is that your soul and money may now play together in the garden of your life.

The seeds that will grow are the seeds you tend with your attention. Your attention is like water and sunshine and the seeds you cultivate will grow and fill your garden.

Recommended Reading

Attwood, Janet Bray and Attwood, Chris. *The Passion Test.*

Plume. Published by The Penguin Group 2008

Bateson, Catherine Mary. *Composing a Life.*

Grove Press, New York. 1989

Bennett, Bija. *Emotional Yoga.*

A Fireside Book. Published by Simon and Schuster 2002

Brunton, Paul. *In Search of India*

1934

Chopra, Deepak. *Creating Affluence: Wealth Consciousness in the Field of All Possibilities.*

Novato, Calif.: New World Library, October 1993.

Desikachar, T.K.V. *The Heart of Yoga: developing a personal practice.*

Library of Congress Cataloging-in-Publication Data. 1995

Fahri, Donna. *Bringing Yoga to Life: The Everyday Practice of Enlightened Living.*

Harper Collins, New York. 2004

Gladwell, Malcolm. *The Tipping Point: How Little Things Can Make a Big Difference.*

Little, Brown, and Co. Time Warner Book Group. 2002

Hanson, Rick Ph.D. *Buddha's Brain, happiness, love and wisdom.*

New Harbinger Publications, Inc. Oakland, CA 2009

Iyengar, B.K.S. *Light on Pranayama. The Yogic Art of Breathing.*

The Crossroad Publishing Company. New York. 2008

Iyengar, B.K.S. *Light on Yoga. The Bible of Modern Yoga- Its Philosophy and Practice by the World's Foremost Teacher.*

Published by George Allen & Unwin Ltd. New York. 1966, 1968, 1976

Johnstone, Chris. *Find Your Power. Boost Your Inner Strengths, Break through Blocks and Achieve Inspired Action.*

Nicholas Brealey Publishing. London and Boston, Maine. 2006

Johnson, Robert and Jerry Ruhl Ph.D. *Living the Unlived Life: Coping with Unrealized Dreams and Fulfilling Your Purpose in the Second Half of Life.*

Penguin. 2007

Kahneman, Daniel and Tversky, Amos. *Choices, Values and Frames.*

Cambridge University Press. 2000

Langer, Ellen. *Mindfulness.*

A Merloyd Book. Da Capo Press. A member of the Perseus Books Group. 1989, 2014

Marti, Molly J.D. Ph.D. *Walking with Justice*

Greenleaf Books 2012

Myers, David G. *Intuition, Its Powers and Perils*

Yale University Press. New Haven and London. 2008

Needleman, Jacob. *Money and the Meaning of Life.*

Published by Doubleday, New York. 1991

O'Neill, Barbara. *How Real People Handle Money 2. 15 more financial planning case studies.*   Jan 1. 1998

Nomura, Catherine and Julia Waller with Shannon Waller; based on a concept by Dan Sullivan. *Unique Ability. Creating the Life You Want.*

Printed in Toronto, Canada. February 2006. The Strategic Coach Inc.

Pert, Candace B. *The Molecules of Emotion: The Science Behind Mind-Body Medicine. Why You Feel the Way You Feel.*

Scribner; 1st edition (September 11, 1997)

Roth, Ganeen. Lost and Found. *One Woman's Story of Losing Her Money and Finding Her Life.*

Viking. Published by the Penguin Group. 2011.

Shefrin, Hersh. *Beyond Greed and Fear: Understanding Behavioral Finance and the Psychology of Investing.*

Oxford University Press. 2002.

Siegel, Daniel, J. Mindsight. *The New Science of Personal Transformation.*

Mind Your Brain Inc. Bantam Books, New York. 2010

Singer, Michael A. *The Untethered Soul Guided Journal. Practices to Journey Beyond Yourself.*

New Harbinger Publications Inc. 2020. Printed in China. Distributed in Canada.

Tindall, Julia. *Your Presence is Enough.*
BookSurge, LLC 2006. CA USA

Tindall, Julia. *20 Questions for Enlightened Living. Peace and Freedom through Jnana Yoga.*
Heaven on Earth Project, Mt Shasta CA. 2003

Tindall, Julia. *The Practice of Presence. 21 commandments for calm and contentment.*
Middletown, DE, USA. 2018.

Tolle, Eckhart. *The Power of Now. A Guide to Spiritual Enlightenment.*
Yoga Impressions (IBD) 2001

Tolle, Eckhart. *A New Earth. Awakening to Your Life's Purpose.*
Plume Published by the Penguin Group. 2006

Upledger, John D.O., O.M.M. *Somato-Emotional Release. Deciphering the Language of Life.*
North Atlantic Books. Florida, 200

Notes:

www.ingramcontent.com/pod-product-compliance
Lightning Source LLC
Chambersburg PA
CBHW071447220526
45472CB00003B/701